Read what the industry is saying about these books:

They fit the way we operate in the 90's. They are fast-paced and packed with hard-hitting tidbits. In just a few minutes, I can pick up a great idea and get back to work!

Greg Hunsucker, Co-owner
V's Italiano Ristorante, Kansas City, MO

What a great idea! I can't tell you how many management books I have started and never finished. These have exactly the sort of information I can really use – concise and to the point.

Mark Sneed, Director of Operations
Phillips Seafood Restaurants, Washington, DC

You can't miss with advice from the best of the best! I like that these books don't preach. They credit me with enough intelligence to be able to adapt these ideas to fit my particular situations. Why didn't somebody do this sooner?

Mark Valente, Owner
Marc's Restaurant, Wheatridge, CO

These books contain practical ideas in an easy-to-read format that can help any operator increase sales, reduce costs and improve profit margins. They are useful books for any food professional from multi-unit director to small kitchen manager.

William Dillon, VP for Market Development
ARAMARK Campus Services, Philadelphia, PA

The Hospitality Masters Series

An invaluable collection of insights and experience from professionals who understand our business . . . filled with some simple "how to" solutions.

Marjorie Mintz, VP Human Resources
The Levy Restaurants, Chicago, IL

A super-concentrated collection of immensely valuable sales and profit-building ideas. These books will be a tremendous resource to anyone in the hospitality industry.

David Newton, Director of Operations
Applebee's, Pittsburgh, PA

These are the perfect resource for busy food & beverage executives. Every page is loaded with common sense that I can put in my managers' hands for quick training of important issues. It's like a total Restaurant University in a book!

Greg Gallavan, F&B Director
Winter Park Resort, Winter Park, CO

As the owner of a restaurant, I am always searching for ways to improve my sales and profit. [These books] are a practical and effective tools for my management staff and myself to use for continual growth and success.

Chris Shake, Owner
The Fish Hopper, Monterey, CA

These books are filled with clear, concise advice that can definitely increase the bottom line. I've read industry books twice the length with half the insights.

Richard Ysmael, Corporate Director
Motorola Hospitality Group, Schaumburg, IL

HOSPITALITY MASTERS SERIES

Tested ideas from the leading speakers and consultants in the hospitality industry

CONTRIBUTING AUTHORS:

Barry Cohen
Award-winning chef, national speaker and CEO of Old San Francisco Steak House

Howard Cutson, FMP
Principal of Cutson Associates and a sought-after speaker on customer satisfaction and beverage operations

Peter Good, FMP
Nationally-recognized motivational speaker and trainer to the hospitality industry.

Raymond Goodman, PhD
The leading authority on dining room management and service management consulting

Jim Laube, CPA
Popular speaker, trainer and consultant on financial management and profitability issues

Bill Main, FMP, FCSI, CSP
Nationally-known author, consultant and speaker and Past President of the California Restaurant Association

Phyllis Ann Marshall, FCSI
Principal of FoodPower, specialist in concept development, growth strategies, and merchandising with food and menus

Bill Marvin, The Restaurant Doctor™
The most-booked speaker in the hospitality industry, author, consultant and advisor to operators around the world

Banger Smith
One of the recognized leaders in menu analysis and merchandising design

Ron Yudd
Director of Food Service for the United States Senate Restaurants and an experienced speaker, trainer and motivator

50 Proven Ways to Build More Profitable Menus

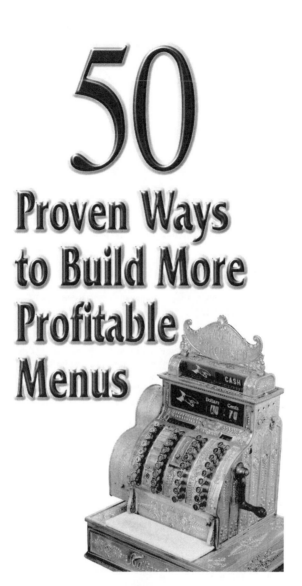

Edited by
William R. Marvin

Hospitality Masters Press
PO Box 280 • Gig Harbor, WA 98335

Other books in the Hospitality Masters Series:

50 Proven Ways to Build Restaurant Sales & Profit
50 Proven Ways to Enhance Guest Service

Printed and bound in the United States of America.

Photo Credits
Page 124 – Sharon A. Pecoraro, Hudson, OH
Page 130 – Stegner Portraits, Colorado Springs, CO

ISBN 0-9656262-4-5

ATTENTION ASSOCIATIONS AND MULTI-UNIT OPERATORS:
Quantity discounts are available on bulk purchases of this book for premiums, sales promotions, educational purposes or fund raising. Custom imprinting or book excerpts can also be created to fit specific needs.

For more information, please contact our Special Sales Department, Hospitality Masters Press, PO Box 280, Gig Harbor, WA 98335, (800) 767-1055, e-mail: info@hospitalitymasters.com, Fax: (888) 767-1055.

CONTENTS

Part 3
PROFIT MECHANICS

Part 4
POINTS TO PONDER

APPENDIX

* originally published in ***50 Proven Ways to Build Restaurant Sales Profit*** and recycled because it is so relevant to the subject of this book

ABOUT THE HOSPITALITY MASTERS SERIES

You may have heard the old exchange:

Q: ***What is the secret of success?***
A: ***Success comes from good judgement.***
Q: ***Well, where does good judgement come from?***
A: ***Good judgement comes from experience.***
Q: ***OK, but where does experience come from?***
A: ***Experience comes from bad judgement!***

The joke would be funnier if it weren't so accurate!

Have you noticed that the School of Hard Knocks has high enrollment? When wrestling with a problem, have you ever wished you could pick the brain of an industry expert who has "been there and done that" instead of just volunteering for yet another "valuable learning experience?"

Well, that is precisely the purpose of the Hospitality Masters Series of books.

We tapped the leading consultants and speakers in the foodservice and lodging industries for their most successful ideas on a series of topics essential to success in hospitality.

Hospitality Masters Press was formed to collect these gems, distilled from years of industry experience with their own (and others') triumphs and tragedies, and present them in bite-sized pieces that even the most harried manager can quickly digest and apply.

The consultants, speakers and authors whose ideas are collected here are the best of the best in our business. At any meaningful gathering of industry leaders in North America, one or more of these experts are probably sharing insights in a standing-room only seminar or workshop.

When the leading operators in the U.S. and Canada look for professional counsel, these are the names on the "short list." Our contributing authors produce the tapes that encourage and inspire thousands and write the books that become standard industry references.

50 Proven Ways to Build More Profitable Menus is the latest in a most valuable and exciting series. We welcome any comments you may have on this book as well as your suggestions for future titles.

We believe the books in the Hospitality Masters Series will become must-have additions to the professional library of every foodservice and lodging executive.

We think you will agree.

INTRODUCTION

Your menu is your blueprint for profit. It determines your image, defines your concept and is the shopping list your guests use to spend their money. Often it is your best (or worst) sales-maker.

What is a menu?
For purposes of this book, we define a menu as any means used to communicate to a guest what a food service operation has to offer. This obviously includes traditional printed menus but can also encompass menu boards, specialty menus, verbal menus, cafeteria menus and catering presentations.

How can a menu be profitable?
The menu does not produce the profit but, properly designed and presented, it can help increase the sales that do! When a menu is poorly designed, guests get confused and order the first thing that comes to their minds. They get about what they expected and may leave satisfied, but they will have spent a minimal amount for a dining experience that will quickly be forgotten. What's wrong with this picture?

However, when a menu is exciting and different, it can catch the guests' attention. They get wrapped up with what you are offering, have a better time and are more likely to try items they never had before. They get more than they expected, leave delighted and spend more money for a dining experience that was more memorable and more likely to cause them to return. ***That*** is how your menu can (and should) be profitable!

About this book

This is not a "how-to" manual. In fact, you may find seemingly contradictory ideas in here. The industry experts we have gathered in this book cannot tell you how you should run your business – the goal is only to share ideas that have worked for others. You must decide which ones, if any, are appropriate for you.

Each thought in this book has been condensed to its bare essence so some may raise more questions than they answer. If this happens, the contributing authors can provide more clarification . . . but only if you ask! Contact information is included in Appendix A.

How to use this book

This book is a collection of bulletproof ideas from battle-tested veterans – use it that way. Keep it close and refer to it often. Ideas you are not ready for today might be perfect answers a few months from now.

Get copies of this book for all key members of your management team and have pass-around copies for your staff. The cost is minimal and the potential gain is huge. (Helping others to make you more money is a very smart thing to do!)

A closing thought

Good ideas won't make you rich – only the ***application*** of good ideas will make life better. This book should make you think. Ultimately, the real power in these ideas may not be in the ideas themselves, but rather in the insights that each may trigger for you. We hope you will adapt these notions to fit your needs and take them to a new level! Good luck!

Part 1

First Things First

1
Menu First

The menu should be the first item to be fleshed out in building a concept because it affects every aspect of the business. No matter what the size, shape or style of the restaurant, the menu is the hub of the operation. The stronger the links are between the menu and all other aspects of the restaurant business, the more powerful, popular and profitable the concept is likely to be and the easier it will be to grow.

The menu affects everything about a restaurant from the name on the front door to the purveyors arriving at the back door. It determines the optimum location, the demographics needed to attract the customer desired.

It determines the design of the building and the decor both inside and out. The menu is the necessary guideline to design an efficient kitchen, to choose the equipment package and to decide on the kitchen staff in terms of both prior experience and training needed.

The menu dictates the style of service and determines the staffing needed to operate the business. It sets the price points, the check average, the operation's day parts and the sales volume necessary for profitability.

Bottom line tip:
A restaurant in the development stage should earmark a budget for detailed menu and recipe development. These documents should be included in the business

plan as they provide the basis to forecast the potential sales of the restaurant and serve as the primary planning guideline for designers and support personnel.

A restaurant undergoing retrofit or redefinition because of low sales volume will also find that the menu is the key to the changes needed to regain profitability. The menu will affect everything from the decor uplift to the new look on the tabletop. It drives any changes in the service, kitchen and basic operation that will determine the new marketing image of the restaurant and the action necessary to implement it.

Everything is linked to the food and menu . . . there is no escaping it. If your heart is not in the kitchen with the food, you must find this passion in an operating partner or a well-paid employee with a performance bonus. A restaurant without a strong sense of its menu (and the kitchen support to deliver it) will find it difficult to survive the aggressive onslaught of national chains and local competition with better food.

Phyllis Ann Marshall and her company, FoodPower, help restaurants mine the gold hidden in their menus. She specializes in merchandising with food and menus. For more details and contact information, see Page 129.

2
The Menu as a Marketing Plan

Whether your restaurant or foodservice facility is a chain or independent, high volume dinner house, fast food chili doggery, casual outdoor bistro or corporate cafeteria, the menu is your immediate connection with your guests.

The menu is the purest expression of your marketing plan. It is the first tangible connection your guests have between their interest in buying (why they are there – to dine, socialize or otherwise have a positive experience) and what you have to sell.

So if true marketing is identifying who your customers are and attempting to meet their needs or satisfy their requirements, then the menu is the link between your food and service and the guests' expectations – it is the bridge between marketing and operations.

- The menu sets the tone for every operation, whether quick service, mid range/casual or fine dining. It determines the need for management, staff and equipment. It affects the profit potential from energy cost to china breakage, from training protocols to comment cards, from table turns to uniform expense.
- The menu is the connective tissue that holds the entire restaurant together. Nothing happens that in some way is not directly (or indirectly) affected by the menu.
- The menu is a translation of the food offered. In a way, the menu is a form of a product brochure.

- The menu is the cornerstone of profitable operations and the centerpiece of the guests' dining experience. It establishes expectations that the food will ultimately have to fulfill and which will, in turn, determine the guests' desire to return.

As an offensive weapon, the menu is, of course, only the means to an end. Every operator's objective, one way or another, is to use the menu to achieve higher sales in one of four ways:

Increase the average check

Encourage and stimulate selection behaviors that result in buying more from the menu per visit.

Increase frequency of visits

The menu's fabulous selections attract more frequent patronage, driving sales upward.

Increase party size

The menu stimulates guests to expand party size to share in the wonderful dining experience.

Attract new patrons

Properly merchandised, the menu is a powerful selling tool to be strategically distributed through appropriate channels to win new converts.

Given these sales building strategies, the menu offers a uniquely flexible and adaptable format to creatively merchandise the food and beverage items available.

This material is excerpted from ***Menu Magic***™ by Bill Main, nationally-known author, consultant, speaker and Past President of the California Restaurant Association. For more details and contact information, see Page 128.

3
Your Menu: Cost or Asset?

Do you think of your menu as a profit-producing asset or as a controllable cost? A menu is the most powerful merchandising tool at an operator's disposal but all too often it functions simply as a decorative price list.

Have you ever been handed a dog-eared, stained, smelly menu in a highly-regarded restaurant? Perhaps an especially appealing item was unavailable because, as the waiter discreetly whispered, "the cost went way up and they can't afford to sell it at that price!" When things like this happen, the tail is wagging the dog – profitability has become subordinate to menu expense.

Just as a successful coach must make frequent player adjustments to stay competitive, a savvy restaurateur must regularly evaluate the mix of sales and gross profit contribution of each item and make frequent changes to maximize profitability. It sounds easy enough but it doesn't happen because it looks like the menu will be too costly to revise. When a menu remains in service too long, like even the finest athlete, it gets tired and productivity (or profitability in this case) suffers.

Why would an otherwise brilliant operator lose hundreds of dollars by holding on to a rigid menu program that makes changes seem cost prohibitive when the dollars spent to revise the menu could probably be recovered in about a week? Because they are thinking cost rather than asset.

A well-designed menu will influence your guests' total purchases, not just the entree, while reflecting and reinforcing the key components of your marketing mix – concept, atmosphere, service, location, image, reputation and value. How much is that worth to you?

Consider a restaurant with annual sales of $500,000, and a $6.00 average check. That means that 83,000 guests will look to your menu for guidance in making choices and receive an impression of your restaurant (and you!) at the same time. An up to date, thoughtfully positioned menu, and a motivated server trained to sell suggestively, will help to ensure a winning recipe for increased profits.

If you begin looking at your menu as the income producing asset that it is, you will be on the right track to greater profitability.

Banger Smith is one of the recognized leaders in menu analysis and merchandising design who says he has never met a menu he couldn't make more profitable! For more details and contact information, see Page 131.

4
What's your PQ?

What is your Profitability Quotient (PQ)? If you answer "no" to any of the following questions, you could be leaving thousands of dollars in gross profit on the table.

1. Do you have an up-to-date, accurate standard recipe manual and is it incorporated into your daily routine?
   Yes ❑ No ❑

2. Do you have an up-to-date, accurate food cost for every item sold on the menu?
   Yes ❑ No ❑

3. Do you know your top 10 selling items on the menu, their costs and gross profit contribution?
   Yes ❑ No ❑

4. Do you review sales mix reports from your point-of-sale system at least weekly?
   Yes ❑ No ❑

5. In your operation, is gross profit margin more important than food cost?
   Yes ❑ No ❑

6. Have you updated your menu in the last 3-4 months?
   Yes ❑ No ❑

7. Do you know what category (i.e., Sandwiches) on the menu is the most popular?
   Yes ❑ No ❑

8. Do you apply a profit strategy to layout and design in all your merchandising materials?
   Yes ❑ No ❑

9. Is your pricing of menu items focused on gross profit contribution?
   Yes ❑ No ❑

10. Do you use "special sheets" to communicate daily specials?
    Yes ❑ No ❑

11. Is your wine list incorporated into your core menu?
    Yes ❑ No ❑

12. Do you know what percentage of your guests order appetizers? beverages? sides? desserts?
    Yes ❑ No ❑

13. Do you train your staff to sell suggestively and track their effectiveness?
    Yes ❑ No ❑

14. Is your menu flexible so you can make changes quickly and inexpensively?
    Yes ❑ No ❑

15. Do you know who your main competitors are?
    Yes ❑ No ❑

16. Do you perform a competitive menu comparison with your direct competition?
    Yes ❑ No ❑

17. Do you involve staff in your menu decisions?
    Yes ❑ No ❑

18. Are your menus and related point-of-purchase material in full color?
    Yes ❑ No ❑

Banger Smith is one of the recognized leaders in menu analysis and merchandising design who says he has never met a menu he couldn't make more profitable! For more details and contact information, see Page 131.

5
Create Menu Diversity

The market is flooded with "me-too" menus that are loaded with such "standards" as chicken Caesar salad, fried cheese sticks and grilled chicken breast.

The only options most of us consider when trying to be different are to 1) discount our items, 2) provide noticeably larger portions or 3) add cute little names to our dishes and claim that they have originality. None of these is particularly appealing to our bottom lines and none produces W.O.W. with our guests.

There is a better option which I call menu diversity – providing customers with choices that no one else can offer them. It sounds easy but it takes a lot of effort. As with any W.O.W. program you implement in your business, menu diversity requires that you be Watchful, Open and Willing. Here's how:

Be Watchful

Look around you're your dining room to see what your guests are eating, What are they asking for that you don't serve? What accompaniments are they adding to their main course on their own? Guests give us clues all of the time, and we usually ignore them. Watch other restaurants also, especially the small places which attract swarms of locals. We flock to the newest and most expensive restaurants for a taste of what's chic, but it is often the small independents who have their fingers on the pulse of the market.

Be Open

For decades, Lawry's Prime Rib prided itself on selling only one entree: prime rib. But today, that's simply not realistic. Too many customers want a healthful alternative. So now Lawry's serves fish. We could all be more open to serving new dishes, or even old ones in more innovative ways. Allow your chefs room to be creative within a strict set of cost and supply parameters. That's what they're paid for more than anything else! If you've hired the right people, they should be eager to bring new ideas to the menu and additional sales to your tables. If you treat your menu as a closed book, you are confining yourself to mediocrity and ultimately to obsolescence.

Be Willing

If you're going to create an innovative menu, you've got to be willing to have faith in your chefs. When I was a chef at a hotel in Florida, our menu was fairly typical. However, I was allowed to play around with it and in the process, came up with coconut shrimp. The dish drew countless diners into our hotel and has since become a standard. Behind every success like fajitas, frozen Marganita or wraps, there were chefs who were allowed to take some risks and owners who were willing to invest some faith in them.

When we try to appeal to the greatest number of people, we tend not to strive for W.O.W., but settle for the lowest common denominator instead. That is a recipe for disaster, not for delighted diners.

Barry Cohen is a Texas-based restaurateur, CEO of Old San Francisco Steak House, the author of ***W.O.W. 2000*** and a national speaker. For more details and contact information, see Page 123.

6
Quick Service Clarity

Guests want to know what you are offering for sale. Many would like to know how the food is prepared. They also want to know the ingredients. How does it look? How do I get it? How much does it cost?

The quick service solution

To answer these questions, quick service restaurants have developed sophisticated systems for the guest to determine their order. Here is some of what they offer:

- back-lighted menu boards that include sizes, prices and full color product photos arranged in categories that are keyed to a color code
- sample menu items on display to help answer customer concerns and questions
- cup and container size displays, point of sale signs and photos at the cash register
- signs designating where to place and pick up orders
- station line indicators, cash register positioning and counter service communication systems
- international signs such as, NO MSG (red circle with a red line through it) and red hearts or vinyl letters with lite to indicate the healthier items
- branded logos to indicate quality

It's not just quick service anymore

The proliferation of quick service and family style dining

establishments with aggressive takeout sections has put the pressure on full service restaurants to provide the same information on the menu and from the server.

Here are a few more concerns your menu should be addressing:

Portion sizes

Older diners are interested either in smaller portion sizes or in larger portions where a portion can be taken home for a second meal.

Health considerations

Many diners are interested in the nutritional content of what they eat, especially the cholesterol or fat content and like to see this information either on the menu or readily available for the asking.

White tablecloth exemption

Visuals are essential in all but the most elegant operations – those where the chef has a famous name and the consumer trusts the restaurant implicitly.

Clarity of concept and menu is the key to customer satisfaction because confusion results in both lost sales and customer stress. Guests are more stressed, tired, confused than ever and they don't need any more hassles in their lives. They like the restaurant to make it easy for them to decide. It is time to reexamine your menu and make sure it is clear and guest-friendly.

Phyllis Ann Marshall and her company, FoodPower, help restaurants mine the gold hidden in their menus. She specializes in merchandising with food and menus. For more details and contact information, see Page 129.

7
Take Your Menu's Temperature

To see if a person is sick, you take his temperature. . . and it is no different with menus. How long has it been since you took your menu's temperature? At Old San Francisco, we give our menu a serious checkup every six months. And every time, we find that there are plenty of things we could be doing better.

We discover that we could be serving new desserts, better cuts of meat on some dishes, or newly popular indulgences like cigars. Then we make changes, because we want our menu to be as hot as our steaks! Here are a few of the questions you should ask when you diagnose your own establishment's menu:

Where is the W.O.W.?

Is your menu's temperature a few degrees above or below that of your competition? Do you offer exciting and different choices or are you beginning to look a little bit tired? The challenge in this business isn't achieving quick success; it's sustaining a loyal flow of customers and sales. You must find new sources of W.O.W. all the time.

What's Selling?

Any restaurant in operation today should have a point-of-sale (POS.) system sophisticated enough to take stock of which items are selling and which are not. Don't make the mistake of thinking you know – use your equipment and get the real numbers at least weekly. I suggest you go one step further and calculate what percentage of your sales are coming from new items on your menu. Guests' tastes change from year to year, and if you are just selling the same plates over and over, you are not keeping up with the times.

What Will Be Trendy Tomorrow?

Any business that simply tried to keep up with the times would find itself with an obsolete product line in short order. The same is true of restaurants. At Old San Francisco, we try to stay at least six months ahead of the curve with new items our guests may not have seen anywhere. For example, we started serving emu and ostrich meats a couple of years ago, even though demand so far is negligible. We had flaming desserts well before the "splurging" trend became apparent. Your menu is a statement of how well you have planned for the future. What does yours say about you?

Are You the Right Size?

In menus, bigger is not necessarily better. Know what you can execute perfectly and consistently and stick to it. Restaurants which offer in incredible range of their menu choices often end up disappointing their guests. Big menus can lead to menu confusion – where what you order is not necessarily what you get. What your server ultimately delivers may be wonderful enough, but if it does not match with the menu description, you have still delivered a disappointing experience.

So what is the temperature of your menu? Now is the time to determine if your menu is ill or healthy. Don't put it off – a sick menu can be life-threatening!

Barry Cohen is a Texas-based restaurateur, CEO of Old San Francisco Steak House, the author of ***W.O.W. 2000*** and a national speaker. For more details and contact information, see Page 123.

8
Think Gross Margin

Most operators can tell you their food cost; many can even give it to you for each menu item. Fascinated with percentages, they design menus to promote sales of the items with the lowest food cost . . . and in so doing, often destroy their profitability!

You can't pay bills with percentages, so achieving the lowest possible food cost may not produce the highest possible profit. Say for example, two of your big sellers are the Southwestern Strip Steak at $15.95 (45% food cost) and the Grilled Seafood Pasta at $9.95 (32% cost). If you are thinking percentages, you would promote sales of the Seafood Pasta. If you are thinking profitability, you would promote the steak.

Here is how it works: Your food cost in the Seafood Pasta is $3.18 (32%) and your gross margin – the dollars you have left to pay the bills after you have put the meal on the plate – is $6.77. The steak has a product cost of $7.18 (45%) but a gross margin of $8.77. So even though you reduce your food cost by selling pasta instead of steak, you also reduce your bottom line by two dollars every time you sell the Seafood Pasta at the expense the Southwestern Strip.

By determining the ingredient costs and gross profit margins of your menu items you dramatically enhance your ability to make more intelligent and profitable menu decisions.

Here are a few of the ongoing menu decisions faced by restaurant operators and why it is to your advantage to know your gross profit margin on each menu item:

- What is the impact on profitability of price changes in your raw products? Your raw product costs, particularly seafood and produce, change all the time. What may have been a profitable menu item two months ago may not be so desirable today and you need to know it.

- What dishes should become your signature items? What do you want to be famous for? Certainly the most popular items are prime candidates to be your signatures . . . but are they also the most profitable?

- What desserts or appetizers should servers suggest first? As long as you're sure the guests will love them, offer the items with the largest gross profit margins!

- What menu items can you afford to discount? In an intensely competitive environment it might make sense to occasionally discount selected menu items. How much of a discount can you afford on selected items and still make a reasonable profit?

- How should the menu be designed? Menu design, placement and graphics will affect selection rates of specific menu items. Gross profit margins can help you determine where to place menu items and how graphic techniques should be used to promote those items with the most impact on your bottom line.

Jim Laube, CPA, is President of the Center for Foodservice Education and a consultant in profitability and financial management. For more details and contact information, see Page 127.

9
Recipe Costing

To be able to build more profitable menus, you (and your kitchen manager and chef) first must be able to perform basic recipe costing based on a recipe and raw ingredient breakdown. It takes time and it is hard work but a restaurant is a manufacturing facility and good manufacturers know their production costs.

This is typically done as a "recipe explosion" and can be done manually or on the computer using general purpose spreadsheet programs or dedicated recipe costing software. Computerization is great, but no matter how you do it, the most important thing is that you break down every recipe into its component parts and accurately determine its total cost.

To develop accurate costs, it is also important that the recipe clearly defines the way the item is to be cooked and presented. You should also document the plate arrangement with a color photo.

This may sound like a lot of detail, but line cooks have a tendency to prepare items just a little differently from the recipe – to add their own individual signature – and this can destroy product consistency. Lack of consistency causes out-of-control product costs and leads to a lack of trust with your guests.

The example on the next page illustrates a properly costed recipe for Scallops Sausalito.

Menu Item Costing Worksheet

Menu: Dinner

Date: 05/02/91

By: S. Gravelle

Item: Scallops Sausalito

Description:

Tender scallops poached in white wine, butter, garlic, shallots, mushrooms and green onions, simmered in a rich Bechamel sauce and served on a bed of rice with fresh vegetables.

Item ID	Quantity	Measure	Ingredient	Unit/Price	Cost
SHE514	1	each	Scallop Portion - 7 oz.	2.60	2.60
SSI1133	4	ounce	Bechamel Sauce	0.08	0.32
DAI115	1	ounce	Butter Solids - unsalted	0.07	0.07
PRO102	2	ounce	Mushrooms - medium	0.15	0.30
PRO113	0.1	bunch	Onions - green	0.03	0.00
PRO137	0.2	ounce	Garlic - fresh	0.03	0.01
PRO154	0.5	ounce	Shallots - fresh	0.03	0.02
WIN100	2	ounce	Wine - white house	0.05	0.10
SSI121	4	ounce	Rice - cooked	0.12	0.48
GRO428	0.1	ounce	Spice - pepper white ground	0.39	0.04
SSI502	1	each	Dinner package	1.50	1.50
				Total Cost	5.44
				Menu Price	15.95
				Food Cost	34.09%

Cooking Procedure:

In sauce pan on medium heat add white wine, scallops, shallots, garlic, mushrooms and salt and pepper (to taste). Simmer until scallops appear white in color, leaving one ounce of liquid in the pan. Add bechamel, green onions and butter then simmer for two minutes more until a medium consistency is reached. Serve in a large ceramic casserole dish on a bed of rice, piling scallop mixture in the middle then pour remaining sauce in pan over the top. Sprinkle lightly with paprika (for color) and serve with fresh vegetables on a large oval platter garnished with orange wheel and sprig of fresh parsley.

So develop that comprehensive book of standardized recipes with clear cooking specifications and plate presentation guidelines. Have an accurate, current costing and stay on top of individual ingredient price fluctuations. Only when you know what each item costs to produce (and more important, what each contributes in gross profit margin) can you truly begin to build more profitable menus.

This material is excerpted from ***Menu Magic***™ by Bill Main, nationally-known author, consultant, speaker and Past President of the California Restaurant Association. For more details and contact information, see Page 128.

10
Menu Analysis

If you do not know what each item on your menu costs, you may be leaving 5% on the table! Easily 90% of all restaurants do not have accurate, up-to-date costs for all the items they sell, let alone know what the individual gross profit contribution (margin) is from each menu item. Without that information, you cannot create a more profitable menu. You need a menu analysis.

To perform a menu analysis, you need the following:

- A computer with some type of spreadsheet or menu analysis software. This can be done manually (see the example in Bill Main's article on the preceding page) but if you can computerize, it makes it easier to stay current as prices change in the future.
- A copy of your menu
- A current product mix (or sales abstract reports) for a minimum of 2-3 periods (months)
- An accurate recipe and food costing for all menu items

Your first step in menu analysis is to review your written recipes. When was the last time your recipes were costed? Most likely they were done when the last menu was written (which on average is every 6-8 months). The people usually responsible for recipe costing (the chefs) are typically busy handling day-to-day operations. They often have little time to spend on the minute details that will make or break your operation.

And the little things will kill you. Your business is about dimes, nickels and pennies. Ask yourself, what a penny is worth? It is only 1/100 of a dollar, yet in a restaurant with annual sales of $1.5 million, being off by one penny is worth $15,000 . . . that isn't "chump change!"

The next step is to analyze your menu, asking two critical questions: Does the menu accurately reflect your concept, goals and position in the marketplace? Is your menu providing you with the maximum gross profit contribution?

Then you must examine every item on the menu for popularity and contribution to gross profit. Each item will fall into one of four distinct categories:

- Menu items that have a high gross profit contribution and high product mix. These items have maximum menu power, and depending upon your menu, these items should command the best real estate on the menu. The more we can influence mix toward these items, the more profitable the operation will be.
- Menu items that sell well (high in product mix) but have less-than-average gross profit contribution. These items are often loss leaders but you've got to have them. Typically, these items are very price sensitive.
- Menu items that have greater-than-average gross profit, but lower-than-average popularity. Sometimes, these items act as "image makers" and provide a largely psychological benefit to the guest. Typically, these are the more expensive items on the menu. Too many of these items can have a negative effect on the menu and they should be candidates for elimination, repackaging, repricing or replacement.

- Menu items that have lower-than-average popularity and make a lower-than-average contribution to gross profit. These items are also candidates for elimination, repackaging, repricing or replacing. If you choose to keep an item in this category, you should know the reason. Often, these items are important to a particular market-segment (like kid's meals) and should stay on the menu to help you remain competitive.

Only when you have all this information can you accurately determine which items should remain on your menu. Only when you have all this information can you make an informed decision about how and where each item should be placed on the menu to have the maximum impact on your profitability.

Conducting a menu analysis is not an easy task, but it is a necessary one that should be performed monthly. However, all the analysis in the world is of no use unless you act upon the information and apply it to your menu. Every month you fail to react and change your menu will cost thousands of dollars in lost profit!

Banger Smith is one of the recognized leaders in menu analysis and merchandising design who says he has never met a menu he couldn't make more profitable! For more details and contact information, see Page 131.

11

Increasing Prices Without Reducing Guest Counts

There is always pressure to increase menu prices, but across the board price increases can decrease the value perceived by the guest and reduce customer counts. It is important to consider all the alternatives before making pricing decisions. There are several ways to achieve greater profitability without wholesale price increases including strategic ("surgical") pricing, menu item placement, product line elimination, product line extensions, promotion and sales staff training.

To illustrate, let me share the experience of a client who recently considered an across-the-board menu price increase and asked for our assistance.

Menu analysis

Our first step was to perform a thorough menu engineering analysis on the menu's sales mix. Next, we recommended items that should be eliminated, repackaged, re-priced, added or merchandised more effectively on the menu.

Of the 34 entree items on the menu, we eliminated four "Dog" (low popularity, low gross profit contribution) entrees, while making a small price increase to nine of the 30 remaining entrees. We also added three new entrees we knew to be more popular and which would produce greater-than-average gross profit.

Merchandising design

To finish the project, we incorporated the menu analysis into the design and layout of the menu, merchandising those items that we considered to be "Stars" (high gross profit, high popularity) and "Puzzles" (higher gross profit, low popularity). We also used design and layout to de-emphasize items considered to be "Plowhorses" (high popularity, low gross profit) and "Dogs" (low in popularity, low in gross profit).

Results

After the introduction of the new menu, the results were incredible! Average gross profit per entree increased $1.74 per guest (13.9%), while the average entree sales price increased $2.07 (9.6%). Through surgical pricing product elimination, product additions, menu design and layout we were able to help increase our client's gross profit more than $7,000 after one period while still maintaining a strong value to the guest.

Most restaurants do not change their menu soon enough because they feel they can't afford it. When they are finally forced to increase prices, it usually ends up being an across-the-board price hike which tends to irritate regular guests. If you think you can't afford to make a change in your menu, ask the client above if he thinks it cost him money to do it!

Banger Smith is one of the recognized leaders in menu analysis and merchandising design who says he has never met a menu he couldn't make more profitable! For more details and contact information, see Page 131.

12
Keep the Menu Alive

A menu and its offerings are a living thing and must constantly be refined and refreshed with new ideas to keep the restaurant (and the bottom line) growing. The best place for those new ideas to come from is the kitchen staff – they are aware of their ability to produce particular dishes, they know the availability of specialty items and they understand the ability of the equipment to produce new "stars" for the menu.

The service staff is also a good resource for new ideas because they listen to customer requests daily. So the service staff knows what they can sell, the kitchen staff knows what they can produce and with a little encouragement and communication they can team up to create wonders. Here are some suggestions:

Stay open to new ideas

Work with the chef and the creative kitchen team on a weekly basis and give them a chance to introduce new ideas, plate presentations, recipes, techniques and products. Visit other good restaurants and welcome new ideas from other staff members. In one restaurant a server approached the chef with the idea of adding souffles to the dessert menu.

Together they tested recipes, decided on flavors and accompanying sauces, organized the service pieces, worked out the ordering procedures and timing. They held a short demo, instruction and tasting for the service staff on kick-off night . . . and sold 100 souffles the first night! The dish is now one of the restaurant's signature items.

Take the creative staff on field trips

Many chefs spend 10-12 hours a day in the same environment working with the same people preparing the same menu using the same ingredients. It can get to be all work with no creative play. To keep the kitchen staff creative, take them out with other talented food people. Consider restaurant and food shows, visits to purveyors, growers and importers and culinary competitions and courses.

This will accomplish three very positive things:

- It will make the kitchen staff feel respected and important to the team.
- It gives you the opportunity to talk with your staff on a more casual basis which will, in turn, help you better understand how they feel about the operation and what ideas they have to make it better.
- It will get their creative juices flowing once again.

Use specials to think outside the box

Encourage new and exciting specials with seasonal or regional themes. Once these ideas are tested as dining room specials, your restaurant team can use the new menu items as a springboard to create signature items, develop retail sales and design special events such as wine dinners and themed holiday celebrations.

Developing this creativity in your staff will usually lead to additional opportunities to create memorable dining experiences and build awareness of the restaurant in the community. These could include off-site catering, participation in chefs' charity events as well as cooking classes and TV demonstrations.

Talk it over

Conduct regular meetings with the entire staff on-site (and occasionally even off-premises) to acknowledge creativity and excellence in both the front and back of the house. Use this time to announce upcoming events, solicit new ideas, volunteer help, explore new sources of business, uncover latent talent and receive staff feedback. These meetings should be a time of discussion and discovery at which the manager is more of a facilitator than a director. The goal is to get (and keep) the entire staff involved and excited.

Successful restaurants require change and innovation. Managers need to keep morale high and sales growing. Chefs need a creative outlet. Servers need exciting new items to offer to diners. Guests need a memorable dining experience, something to tell their friends and the press needs something to shout about. By keeping your menu alive, everyone gets what they need!

Phyllis Ann Marshall and her company, FoodPower, help restaurants mine the gold hidden in their menus. She specializes in merchandising with food and menus. For more details and contact information, see Page 129.

Part 2

The Spice of Life

13
W.O.W. Menus

When was the last time you actually remembered a menu? Chances are that you can't recall a single one. The vast majority of menus look exactly the same. As a result, most of us are boring our customers to indifference by presenting them with monotonous pages of products and prices that inform rather than delight. The answer? Create W.O.W. menus. Here are some of our best ideas from Old San Francisco:

Guest Chef Menus

Chefs used to be no-name kitchen laborers, now they are national and local celebrities. In Texas alone, one of our local chefs has sold more than 200,000 copies of his cookbook! He and others are frequent guests on radio and television shows, teaching people the lost art of cooking. Adding a well-known chef's name to your menu can be an incredibly effective way to get people in the door, as well as to W.O.W. existing customers with a new experience.

Winemaker Menus

In our segment of the industry, guests have gained an increasing interest in simple pleasures such as wines and cigars – pleasures which greatly enhance the dining experience. Why not allow the makers of your most popular wines to create a special menu for certain nights, customized to the enjoyment of their wines? You teach your customers how to create a more enjoyable experience; in the process, you also gain additional beverage sales.

Holiday Menus

At Old San Francisco, Christmas and Thanksgiving are two of our busiest days. We create special menus for these days, as well as for Mother's Day, Father's Day, Valentine's Day and virtually every other holiday where our customers want to W.O.W. a loved one. Sometimes, holiday menu changes are minor, like adding a special dessert. In other cases, we offer a fixed price menu with only a few very special items.

Ethnic Menus

The trend away from traditional American fare is moving our guests toward more diverse dining options. Witness the popularity of fusion cuisines, as well as market acceptance of more authentic bistros and cafes. A successful Mexican restaurant in Dallas recently added a Salvadoran menu and it is packed every night! They did not give up their core business, but now they appeal to an entirely new segment.

Seasonal Menus

Fine-dining restaurants traditionally change menus with the season to take advantage of fresh fruits and vegetables. Now even quick-service restaurants and large casual dining chains have seasonal menus or seasonal items. Especially in areas where weather changes are dramatic, keeping your menu mix the same from season to season is a recipe for leaving your customers in the cold when you should be keeping them warm, or vice-versa.

Break menu monotony and you will help create a more memorable dining experience for your guests.

Barry Cohen is a Texas-based restaurateur, CEO of Old San Francisco Steak House, the author of ***W.O.W. 2000*** and a national speaker. For more details and contact information, see Page 123.

14
Create Menu Magic

At Old San Francisco, our menus tell more than just the description and price of the products we serve – they tell the story of a famous nineteenth-century socialite named Gussie Lee ("the toast of San Francisco") whose lover disappeared on the verge of building the first Old San Francisco Steak House after hearing of her stage coach's ambush by Indians (and therefore her death) nearly 100 years ago.

Irrelevant? Not at all. The legend of Gussie Lee has helped us create a legendary chain of restaurants which have entertained guests for thirty years. Of course, not every restaurant can claim a torrid love affair as its inspiration but every one has a magical story to tell – how the owners became passionate about creating their own space for customers to enjoy, how the town they live in came to be or what each customer means to the community at large. Stories bring magic to your menu but what story do you want to tell?

Nostalgia

The Pioneer Saloon in Sun Valley, Idaho (more often known as the "Pio") tells a nostalgic tale on its menu. Since most of its customers are not locals, The Pio's menu recalls the trek of the first pioneers who set out across the great plains and landed in what is now known as Ketchum, Idaho. In the process, all of the restaurant's meals and ingredients are tied in with the exploits of those first pioneers. So rather than just ordering a steak and a baked potato, customers are ordering a magical trip to the past of the Wild West.

Community Involvement

Starbucks Coffee faced a dilemma: as a quick service operator, it does not have a menu per se. But the company still wanted a space to educate customers about why they were a magical place and not just another coffee bar. One of their important stories was the company's history of community involvement in remote regions of the world where it buys most of its raw coffee. So they created a series of smaller menus detailing, among other things, its support of a charity called C.A.R.E that helps educate young people in Africa, East Asia, and Central America. The story also helps educate patrons about why they should choose Starbucks time and again.

Quality

Morton's of Chicago does a great job of creating magic as well. Rather than hand diners a menu, their servers produce a display of raw product – meats, fish and vegetables – for guests to inspect before they order. This underscores Morton's commitment to superior quality and makes a terrific impact when the steak arrives (magically) cooked to perfection.

So what would work in your operation? How can you go beyond what is expected to give your guests a little magic for their money?

Barry Cohen is a Texas-based restaurateur, CEO of Old San Francisco Steak House, the author of ***W.O.W. 2000*** and a national speaker. For more details and contact information, see Page 123.

15
Upscale Menu Personality

The menu reflects the personality, style and operating philosophy of the restaurant. This is expressed in the type of paper, layout, colors, format, font style, item descriptions, design and cost of the menu.

High end restaurant menus typically have a muted, formal invitation style all of their own. They are generally food, kitchen and chef driven. Food quality and creativity are of prime importance. Therefore the menu needs to be easily changed, generally daily, to take advantage of daily specials, seasonal foods, chefs' creativity and guest expectations.

The menu production costs are concentrated on a permanent cover, if any, with removable light menu pages. The insert pages are often logo-ed stationary that can be run through the computer. Often they include the date and the name of the chef.

The menu highlights selections of meats, fish, poultry and produce that are from either special sources, in limited supply or which help create a signature quality statement. Upscale menus almost always feature signature items – items that are specialties of the chef, specialties of the concept and/or guest favorites that have become so popular that you can't take them off the menu. Sometimes the press has made stars of these items but they are the products you are famous for, which you do better than anyone else in town.

In the best of these restaurants the design component is well planned by a professional in design. The menu is uncluttered, leaving "white space" for effect and balance. The colors are muted and never primary, the price numbers are small and often rounded off to the dollar. There are no boxes, no highlighted areas, no exaggerated designs or prose – just straightforward food, ingredient and preparation descriptions.

Good menus of this type are easy to read, restful on the eyes drawing the guests attention to the food and tantalizing them with promised beauty of presentation and exquisite quality of flavors. The basic premise is that the food speaks for itself.

A great upscale restaurant with a highly talented chef generally has a menu with balance – a couple of signature items that are popular (and profitable) surrounded by other menu items that reflect the heart of the concept. An upscale menu provides its definition with highly innovative, trendy ingredients, combinations or presentations that are new, experimental and often on the edge.

Phyllis Ann Marshall and her company, FoodPower, help restaurants mine the gold hidden in their menus. She specializes in merchandising with food and menus. For more details and contact information, see Page 129.

16
Midscale Menu Personality

In midscale chain restaurants, the creative talent is usually concentrated at the corporate test kitchen level. The written menus are highly creative with a permanent texture that is durable and easy to keep clean. The menus are not changed very often (due to the expense) and the prices are averaged to withstand all but the worst cost fluctuations.

Midscale menus are typically on heavy paper and either laminated or presented in plastic menu sleeves. The colors are bright often a combination of primary and secondary colors and have clever names and images that evoke humor, excitement and interest. The menu engineering is more obvious with boxes, illustrations, branding, icons, photographs and a profusion of color combinations.

The benefits of a midscale concept are that all of the kitchen operations are more basic. A chef is not required in the kitchen, the kitchen staff do not need the skill level of an upscale restaurant, the purchasing is standard and the inventory lower. A midscale concept is easier to duplicate and grow and consistency of the menu items is easier to achieve.

Gimmicks abound to add to the fun and interest. A good midscale menu is pleasantly cluttered but easy to read. It is exciting and playful rather than restful and subdued. The wording of the menu items is often cleverly categorized with trendy names and illustrations and often features extra large portions, larger-than-normal images and artful, over the top combinations.

The menu borrows the most popular, trendy items from the high end restaurants, but reduces them to the basic elements. A midscale restaurant will simplify the ingredients and mute the flavors so that the majority of their guests can identify with the item. The premise of a midscale menu is that the food is designed to appeal to a wide spectrum of the population with a basic, mainstream palate.

Phyllis Ann Marshall and her company, FoodPower, help restaurants mine the gold hidden in their menus. She specializes in merchandising with food and menus. For more details and contact information, see Page 129.

17
Quick Service Menu Personality

Quick service restaurants, coffee shops and diners need bolder messages. They should use very clean primary colors and basic designs that can be illustrated with just a few lines. Boldly contrasting colors (red, white, black) help demonstrate cleanliness.

Speed in decision-making is of primary importance so everything must be basic, simple, uncluttered, clear, and direct. Menu items are often bundled into meal deals with emphasis on price and value. Dramatic stimulation is essential with neon, brightly color food photographs and giant real food images. Menu and merchandising engineering is of prime importance. Every square inch counts.

The less expensive the food, the more the restaurant must depend on volume sales and the more money is typically spent on the menu – typically colorful, heavy, laminated menus with a great many food photos. The colors are bright and primary with bold commercial designs similar to what one would see in advertising for consumer food products.

Quick service operations often utilize a menu board and point-of-sale signs to present their offerings. Major factors in the effectiveness of menu boards and signs are clarity and readability – if guests find a message difficult to read or confusing, they will either take a longer time to make up their minds, default to their old favorites (and make a minimal order) or take their business elsewhere.

Clarity is enhanced by keeping messages simple and using color-coded categories on the menu board. Readability is a function of contrast and letter size with white and yellow letters on a dark background being the most readable. The chart below shows the readability distances for various sizes of letters. Keep it in mind when designing menu boards and other signage.

LETTER VISIBILITY CHART

LETTER HEIGHT	READABLE DISTANCE FOR MAXIMUM IMPACT	MAXIMUM READABLE DISTANCE
¾"	6'	20'
1"	10'	35'
2"	20'	75'
3"	30'	100'
4"	40'	150'
5"	50'	175'
6"	60'	200'
8"	80'	350'
9"	90'	400'
10"	100'	450'
12"	120'	525'
24"	240'	1000'
36"	360'	1500'
48"	480'	2000'
60"	600'	2500'

Courtesy of Signage Solutions, Anaheim, California

Phyllis Ann Marshall and her company, FoodPower, help restaurants mine the gold hidden in their menus. She specializes in merchandising with food and menus. For more details and contact information, see Page 129.

18
Think Combination Menus

In an effort to keep printing costs low, many operators try to make one menu do all the work. While you can make an intellectual case for this, it is short-sighted and can actually reduce volume. Instead, consider the power of using combination menus to build sales and help guests have a more pleasant experience.

The problem
When you throw too much at your guests, whether by handing them several menus at once or leaving a menu that reads like a small novel, they get confused. You also load them down with information they cannot use at the moment. For example, most people will not order dessert at the same time they order appetizers or entrees, yet most menus list both of these categories.

The alternative
Never waste time solving a problem you can eliminate, so why not consider the case for specialty menus? Here is how it might work:

Appetizer/Drink (A/D) menu
When guests are first seated, the first thing you will typically ask them for is an order for appetizers and drinks. Often folks will pass on an appetizer because they are also considering what they will have for a main course. Why not take the pressure off? When guests are first seated, provide them with a small A/D menu highlighting only your appetizer and drink selections.

Entree/Wine (E/W) menu

When servers have asked for the appetizer/drink order, they can take the A/D menu and leave the entree/wine menu that lists the day's main and side dishes and suggests wines to accompany each. Even if the server does a verbal presentation, the specials (featured items, not-on-the-menu items) should be included on the "fresh sheet" in the E/W menu. If your wine selection is extensive, a separate wine list may be in order but you will find that most diners will order wine off the E/W menu if the selections are interesting.

Dessert/Cordial (D/C) menu

At the end of the meal, when you want diners thinking about a sweet finish, bring the dessert/cordial menu. The server hands the D/C menu to guests after clearing the meal plates, perhaps with an aside like, "Take a few minutes to look over our great desserts and after-dinner treats. I'll be right back to give you a few personal recommendations."

The D/C menu gets the diners focused on dessert and gives them something to do until the server can return to the table. It also avoids the need to bring the large entree menu just to show them after-dinner choices. Even if they do not order a dessert, they will have been exposed to your selection which may make a sale easier on their next visit.

So when you think about new menus, think in terms of combinations. The math is easy:

A/D+E/W+D/C=HS (high sales)+HG (happy guests)

Bill Marvin, The Restaurant Doctor is, we suspect, the most-booked speaker in the hospitality industry. At the least, he is a prolific author and advisor to operators across the country. For more details and contact information, see Page 130

19
Mini Menus Offer Leverage

You can add more guest options without substantially adding to either your inventory or your labor by creating specialty or mini-menus. Here are a few menu formats that can expand sales, improve guest satisfaction, update the concept and build the bottom line.

- **Ala carte menus** offer guests just what they want, lets them devise their own combinations and eliminates the old soup or salad choices that force guests to eat a certain way. These menus can move guests from white wine to Chardonnay and from coffee to cappuccino.
- **Combination menus** offer guests both ala carte selections, perhaps with small or large plates, as well as meal packages with an entree and a starter course.
- **Prixe fixe menus** offer three or more courses with a couple of options for one price. This is a wonderful technique for establishing price value and speaking to the complaint of prices that are too high.
- **Breakfast and brunch menus** allow a restaurant with the right demographic to expand into new day parts often without increasing kitchen labor.
- **Afternoon tea menus** are trendy and can be a profit center if there is retail support or a market consisting of tourists, leisurely shoppers or ladies who utilize private party facilities for showers and the like.
- **All day menus** are profitable in a highly visible, heavy trafficked location where there are shifts of employees commuting.

- **Banquet menus** make it easy on the guest needing to make a decision that affects others. Keep them simple – a few packaged favorites and a small list of custom-designed choices as substitutions or add-ons.

- **Catering menus** are similar to banquet menus. Guests need to be directed – they are not very creative when it comes to knowing what you can do. Include address, phone, FAX, and name of the contact person.

- **To go menus and delivery menus** need to be clear, easy to read and quick to decipher the options. Be sure to include your address, phone and FAX.

- **Wine lists** should be appropriate to the operation. A large list only works where the staff and managers are well-versed in the wines. Numbering wines makes it easy for the guest but lowers the operation's image.

- **Special bar menus** have increased the sale of highly profitable beverages like martinis and premium call brands of barrel-aged whiskies. They also add to the image and style of the restaurant.

- **Coffee & tea menus** offer specialty coffees, espresso, cappuccino and combinations with liquors as well as new world teas, bottled teas and waters.

- **Children's menus** allow the parents to know the item prices and choose an appropriate item for their child . . . and for the youngster to use as an amusement.

- **Special language and braille menus** must be professionally translated but are great tools for creating satisfaction and loyalty with special groups.

Phyllis Ann Marshall and her company, FoodPower, help restaurants mine the gold hidden in their menus. She specializes in merchandising with food and menus. For more details and contact information, see Page 129.

20
Develop Signature Appetizers

No discussion of creative menu development would be complete without looking at the power of tabletop merchandising – the table tent – alternately loved and hated by operators in every segment of the industry.

There is nothing particularly trendy or noteworthy about table tent merchandising . . . unless you put a totally different promotional spin on the idea. The new spin is the signature appetizer – an item created and designed to be perfectly suited for sharing by the entire party at the table, whether a couple sharing a romantic evening, a fun-loving family or business executives at work.

Your signatures must be items with universal appeal which guests cannot find anywhere else and are unlikely to prepare at home. The signature appetizer must be so wonderful, so delicious and so connected with the spirit of sharing that it is an automatic order.

Developing signature appetizers is a challenge to both your creativity and your merchandising skills. Whether you list them on the menu or present them on the table tent, here are a few ideas to get you started:

- Keep the table tent simple (no more than two signature appetizers) and affordable (approximately 30-35% of the average entree price). Gear the product toward a large portion for presentation – lots of food, easy to eat, fun to share and a great perceived value.

- Use color and upbeat graphics. Make sure the plastic table tent holder is new and shiny. If possible, use a unique shape – something different and visually interesting that will catch the guest's eye.

- Place the signature appetizer table tent in the middle of the table, directly in the line-of-sight of as many of the group's dinners as possible. Make the patron or guest pick it up to make room for their beverage.

- When parties are being seated, suggest a signature appetizer for the table to share. The table tent can be used as a prop. This simple prompting can increase incremental sales before the food server or cocktail waitress even arrives at the table!

- If the initial contact does not elicit an order, suggest a sampling. Have the kitchen prepare a small plate – a sampler – to offer to guests on a complimentary basis. No more than a taste, this approach will "nudge" at least one-third of the party to request a full order.

The trend toward signature appetizers recognizes the importance of keeping entree prices low while building profitable check averages through aggressive tabletop merchandising and subtle suggestive selling.

This material is excerpted from ***Menu Magic™*** by Bill Main, nationally-known author, consultant, speaker and Past President of the California Restaurant Association. For more details and contact information, see Page 128.

21
Bar Food

"It's more fun to eat food in a bar than to drink in a restaurant."

That comment has been around for years but it is more true today than ever before. The dining public wants to be more casual – jackets, ties and high heels are out when folks go out – and the bar is more comfortable and casual than most dining rooms. Once you grasp that the feel of the bar fits your guests' needs perfectly, you must then learn to maximize the food sales a bar room can generate.

Bar menus are a must

A bar snack menu is a must, just make sure it offers uncomplicated, simple-to-eat, interesting foods. The presentations must be visually exciting, the portions must be large enough to encourage sharing and the selections should not require a knife. Fingers are the best utensils in a bar – a fork only if you must – and don't forget plenty of napkins.

Make the menu exciting with bright colors and big print. Laminate the menus (make sure they get wiped off daily) and get them out on every table and across the bar before you open. If they stand up on their own, all the more obvious. Incorporate those great specialty drinks, micro brews and espresso-based hot drinks. Many vendors offer help with bar menus today so there is no reason not to have a great one!

Visual excitement

Use unique serving dishes. Who says a dish has to be a dish? How about a wicker basket, a cast iron skillet, an old-fashioned carnival french fry cone, a plastic pail, a frisbee, a schooner glass, a flower pot . . . the more unique, the more your guests will remember it and you!

If you must use china, make it colorful, different and unique. Use blacks, reds and loud patterns. Use something that is traditionally used for something else. How about an oversized coffee mug for Vegetable Tempura or a banana split dish for your calamari?

Make it interactive and entertaining

With all the great new cooking equipment available today – like self-contained, no-hood deep fryers and miniature impinger ovens – there's no reason you can't bring the cooking action to the barroom itself. A professional-looking chef in a well-organized, colorful, open work station is the best bar menu you can have!

Remember the piano bars of the 50s? Well, appetizer bars are here for today. Your guests can't miss those great foods headed for neighboring tables and bar stools. The extra sales will more than pay for the labor involved and the product will be outstanding – fresh and hot! (. . . and your servers will sell more because they don't have to stand in line in the kitchen!)

Howard Cutson is Principal of Cutson Associates, a customer service-focused consulting firm specializing in bar operations and creative service training. For more details and contact information, see Page 124.

22
The Specialty Drink Menu

Do you want to boost your beverage alcohol sales by 30-50%? If you will take the time and expend the effort to create a truly exciting drink menu, you can sell more beverages, control inventories, raise check averages and build more satisfied guests at the same time. (And you can even get some assistance from your suppliers if you ask 'em!)

Here are some key factors to keep in mind when designing specialty drink menus:

Stay focused
Remember your overall concept and the clientele you want to attract. What are your guests currently drinking and how can you upgrade those drinks? Could you make that Margarita a "Gold Standard Vodkarita?" Could your Bloody Mary become a "Hot-as-You-Can-Make-It Mary?" You want drinks that fit your concept and are memorable to your guests.

Build in the Ooh! factor
Give each drink a colorful name and a tantalizing description. Don't forget the classic cocktails – they are making a big comeback! Use interesting, distinctive glassware and colorful, fresh, oversized garnishes. You want drinks to draw attention when they are carried through the room. Listen for guests saying, "Ooh! I want one" or asking, "Ooh! What's that?" Look for a spontaneous positive reaction when the drink is placed

in front of the guest. If you are not hearing those "Ooh!" comments, rework your drink presentations until you do!

Be realistic

When you develop your menu, keep in mind the skills of your bartenders and the limitations of your bar equipment. Drinks that take too long to get from the bar or are inconsistently prepared just will not be suggested to the guest!

Integrate the drink list

The best way to sell more drinks is to build the drink list into your food menus. Include pre-dinner suggestions on the appetizer menu. Devote a portion of your dinner menu to the wine list. Build an after-dinner drink library into your dessert menu. This way your guests will be thinking of their beverage choices when they are making their food selections. Now if your service team remembers to simply recommend their favorites . . .

By the way, have you ever sat at the bar of a Planet Hollywood and watched the service bartender? Every other order is one of their signature drinks . . . at prices ranging from $5.50 to $13.95! Wouldn't you like a piece of ***that*** action?

Howard Cutson is Principal of Cutson Associates, a customer service-focused consulting firm specializing in bar operations and creative service training. For more details and contact information, see Page 124.

23
Alcohol-Free Alternatives

At a time when overall alcohol sales are virtually flat, smart operators are creating increases in beverage sales by capitalizing on the hot no-alcohol category. We have seen clients take alcohol-free sales to more than 10% of total sales with very little effort! Here are a few thoughts to help you maximize no-alcohol revenue:

Virgin specials
How about alcohol-free versions of your best-selling signature drinks? Whether kids, nondrinkers or designated drivers, everybody likes something special – the alcohol content is not required. Bonus: selling a special drink instead of soft drinks or coffee keeps you from having to offer those expensive free refills!

N/A beers and wines
These are a must-have category! Carry at least one American label and one import on your menu – more is better. Your staff will get questions, so be sure they have tried the products and can describe them clearly.

Coffee
Coffee is hot (no pun intended!) Get serious about it! Use high-quality beans and grind them immediately before brewing. Use colorful, oversized cups. Offer a selection of special and flavored blends. Don't just serve coffee, develop a coffee ***program.*** In most markets, an espresso machine is still one of the best investments you can make – provided your staff is well-

trained in product knowledge and correct brewing procedures.

The key to coffee sales growth is guest education. To reduce the fear of trying something new, offer a card entitling guests to ten specialty coffee drinks for the same price as a regular cup of coffee. Once they understand the difference, they will be hooked!

Teas

Don't forget about tea! Offer a selection – flavored, decaf, herbal, hot, iced, spiked, bottled, freshly-brewed, make-your-own, etc. You will greatly improve guest satisfaction and add to incremental sales.

Juices

How about fresh-squeezed juices – orange, lemon, lime, grapefruit? What about pineapple, mango and even papaya? They create a quality image, give your drinks a distinctive flavor profile and even add color to your back bar. The premium that you can charge for them adds up as well!

Water

Most servers still pour ice water before attempting to sell an alternative. Offer a selection of bottled waters at reasonable prices and you will be surprised what you can move – still waters, sparkling waters, spring waters, glacial waters, flavored waters, imported waters and hundreds more! Mention the options before just automatically reaching for the water pitcher!

Howard Cutson is Principal of Cutson Associates, a customer service-focused consulting firm specializing in bar operations and creative service training. For more details and contact information, see Page 124.

24
Start a Late Night Menu

What kind of business are you doing late in the evening? If you are like most operators, the answer is probably, "Not much." How about developing a late night meal segment to turn those wasted hours into increased volume?

A successful example of developing the late night trade comes from my current-favorite-restaurant-on-the-planet, Sunset Grill in Nashville, Tennessee. The owner, Randy Rayburn, has implemented a late night menu that has come to exceed lunch as a source of revenue. Best of all, he has accomplished this without expending a penny in advertising!

His late night menu consists of some lower food cost entrees off his regular menu and any items he wants to run out. These entrees are offered at half price from 10:00pm until 1:30am during the week and from midnight until 1:30am on Saturday night. Desserts, coffees and beverages remain at full price.

His late night sales mix is equally divided between food and beverages. Because of its structure, the late night menu only runs about four points higher in overall food cost than his regular menu.

A large percentage of Randy's late night market has become restaurant people looking for a bite to eat in different surroundings when they get off work! His staff makes it a point to inform guests about the late night deal and they, in turn, pass the word along to others. The late night menu takes a smaller kitchen staff to produce and all managers are cross-trained on pantry operations so they can cover in case a kitchen worker calls in sick.

Interestingly, Randy discontinued his early bird program when the late night menu took off. It seemed that the market could think of Sunset Grill either as a place to go early or late . . . but not both.

In Randy's case, he preferred the later business. His early evening business was building up well without any additional incentives and he found that his early diners were not particularly price-driven.

This article was adapted with permission from the book ***Guest-Based Marketing*** by Bill Marvin, The Restaurant Doctor. For more details and contact Information, see Page 130.

25
Dignify Desserts

There is always room for dessert – it is only the ***idea*** of dessert that gives guests pause. It is interesting that many diners will carefully order low calorie entrees and follow up with a massive dessert! You can most always sell a dessert for two diners to split, provided you can capture their imagination. Here are a few ideas about how you might do it.

Create signature desserts

Offer signature desserts – items so unique and mouth-watering that your diners just can't refuse. Present them either in person with a dessert tray or in heartfelt word pictures. Assume that nobody can pass up your special peach cobbler. Back this up with an attractive dessert menu.

Put a candle on the dessert tray

Most dessert trays, no matter how attractive the plates, are still a little flat. Another problem, particularly in the evening, is that the desserts can be a little hard to see. To solve both problems and add a more festive touch, simply put a small candle on the tray.

Housemade desserts

Baking is a lost art at home. Exceptional signature desserts baked fresh on the premises are a major point of difference in the market. If you cannot bake your own desserts, personalize a purchased product with a signature sauce, fresh fruit or something unusual. Don't just cut the cheesecake and put it on a plate.

Speaking of cheesecake, you can give your desserts (and any other item, for that matter) more "talking power" by identifying the source of the recipe. If there is not a good story to tell, name it for the person who made it. ("Joan's Cheesecake" sounds much more interesting than "New York Style Cheesecake.")

Dessert samplers

One of Randy Rayburn's more successful offerings at the Sunset Grill in Nashville is the dessert sampler. Guests can order smaller portions of three or five different desserts attractively displayed on a mirror tray. He says that people love to have a choice and hate to make a decision, so diners who might otherwise say no to a single dessert will say yes to a sampler. An additional advantage is that guests get to try more of Sunset Grill's superb desserts and are more likely to order them the next time they come in.

Extensive dessert wine selection

Consider adding a selection of dessert wines to your menu. They satisfy the need for sweetness, are interesting alternatives to cordials and can be a workable alternative for guests who don't order dessert. As the market develops, so does the variety of wines available, many of which are truly surprising. When you can turn your guests on to something new and wonderful, it makes them feel like pioneers, gives them something to tell their friends about and establishes more of a personal connection with your restaurant.

This material was adapted from a list of more than 200 delightful practices in the book, ***Guest-Based Marketing*** by Bill Marvin, The Restaurant Doctor. For more details and contact information, see Page 130.

26
The User-Friendly Wine List

The more user-friendly you make the wine list, the more product gets ordered and consumed. People want to know what to order to best enhance their dining experience and they depend on you and your team to be the experts – purveyors of knowledge as well as product. Just don't make the learning too difficult, intimidating or potentially embarrassing.

Thoreau knew the right answer:

Simplify! Simplify! Simplify!

Make your wine selection as easy to use as your food menu. Here are a few suggestions:

Make it available

Unless you have a huge wine library in a bound book, make it part of your menu. Even if your servers forget to suggest a bottle, the guest might stumble on the list and order a bottle. Even if you do have that bound list, make sure you offer a "Top 20" list of your most popular selections. Not everyone wants to search for the Pinot Blanc chapter on page 783!

Keep it current

With computers and laser printers, there is no reason for your wine list to ever be outdated – you can rewrite it daily with minimal time and effort. When selections are out-of-stock, you lose the guests' confidence as well! If you are a good customer, a purveyor should protect you on vintage dates for several months. If they refuse, do business with someone who will! There are too many good wines out there to let your reputation suffer from outages.

Make it informative

A well-written wine list should include the grape variety or proprietary name of the wine, the name of the producer, the region and/or country of origin, the vintage date (if any) and a few words of description (fruity, light, full-bodied, oaky) to give the guest a hint as to how it will fit their tastes. Even better, match the wines to your menu items. (Be sure your chef and service team have tasted the food and wine together!) To sell even more wine, suggest a wine or two after each food item on the dinner menu. It eliminates the need to even search for the wine list!

Offer a variety of sizes

Many guests who may feel uncomfortable ordering a full bottle would order a glass – or even a half bottle – of good wine. The more business people you have using your restaurant, the more by-the-glass and half bottle offerings you need to offer. Put them right on the menu or the daily specials sheet. Most guests check that sheet before they move to the regular menu and many never go any further! When you list by-the-glass options, don't forget tasting flights – 2-4 small glasses of several wines at a reasonable price. It is a painless way to learn about wines and your guests will love you for it!

Howard Cutson is Principal of Cutson Associates, a customer service-focused consulting firm specializing in bar operations and creative service training. For more details and contact information, see Page 124.

27
Wine List Weirdness

A menu by any other name is still a menu. Wine lists may be the object of intense study, an afterthought prepared by a salesman or somewhere in between. A full discussion of wine list design is an entire book so for now, here are a few common errors to avoid:

No wine descriptions

Unless your guests are wine experts (and most are not) they may need some help in choosing wines that are unfamiliar to them. Wine lists are typically arranged by color, import/domestic and sometimes by the type of grape. This is a start but it is of little help to those unversed on the wines you offer. Guests understand the differences between sweet and dry wines. Full-bodied and delicate are distinctions they can grasp.

If your patrons are generally wine illiterate, consider restructuring your wine list along these lines. A good wine list encourages patrons to experiment and makes them more comfortable ordering wine. The more comfortable your guests become with wines, the more they will develop the habit of drinking wine with the meal and the better their dining experience will be.

Lack of balance

Effective wine lists offer something for all tastes. Specific requirements for cellar composition depend on your menu. A steak house wine list would likely offer more red wines than a seafood restaurant where the wine list would feature more white wines.

Balance requires a range of choices between red and white, sweet and dry, full-bodied and delicate. Balance also requires a graduated range of prices with selections for every budget. Having your best-selling wines available by the glass is also a plus.

More than three items not in stock

If you are going to offer it, you have to stock it. Maintaining a wine list is a continual process. The more extensive the list, the more time required to support it. This is an area where desktop publishing can help you present a more professional face to the public by allowing you to update your wine list as your inventory shifts. If you cannot reprint the list as wines or vintages change, choose wines where you can count on a reliable supply for an extended period.

Few moderate-priced selections

Many operators price themselves out of the market by trying to price wine with the same percentage markup they use for liquor at the bar. Wine is the only item in the restaurant that you present in the same form as your guests can purchase it themselves. If they know they can buy a particular wine for $10 at the wine shop, they will resent your trying to sell the same bottle for $35. Reasonably priced wines will increase wine sales. Higher sales bring in more dollars and dollars are the way you pay the bills.

A pricing formula you might consider is to start with the ***retail*** price of the bottle (your price, of course, will be less than retail) then add a standard dollar amount, perhaps $5-$7, to provide your profit. The sales price will be fair, higher-priced wines will be more of a bargain and your reputation will spread, favorably, among local wine lovers.

Too many selections

Like menus, wine lists can have so many choices that they become a full time study in themselves. Carefully created and maintained wine cellars are a delightful enhancement of fine dining. Those restaurants with the clientele and staff to appreciate and maintain the wine list, make a special contribution to our industry. For most operators, though, the care and feeding of an extensive wine list can be a struggle, complicated when there are many not-in-stock items.

The wine list is a complement to the restaurant's food menu. Most casually-themed restaurants will be well served by a modest list that is within their ability to understand and service. More upscale restaurants can justify a more extensive list. Many operators at the lower end of the market can make due with interesting house wines. As with any menu, the attraction of a wine list is not what you write but what you can deliver.

This article was adapted from the book ***Restaurant Basics: Why Guests Don't Come Back and What You Can Do About It,*** by Bill Marvin, The Restaurant Doctor. For more details and contact information, see Page 130.

Part 3

Profit Mechanics

28
Sales Mix: A Potent Profit Tool

Monitoring your sales mix on a regular basis will give you a valuable tool that can assist you in eliminating menu losers while enhancing the winners. The sales mix helps you analyze what your guests like and dislike about your menu, tells you what items are selling, what price points are most popular and provides valuable data for future menu decisions.

A sales mix is simply a record of sales per menu item that shows how the items in each category relate to one another. To illustrate, here is a sample sales mix for a four-item appetizer menu:

ITEM	SELL	NO.SOLD	SALES
Nachos	$6.95	10	$ 59.50
Buffalo wings	$5.95	15	104.25
Mini pizza	$5.50	15	82.50
Spinach dip	$4.95	20	99.00
TOTALS		60	$345.25

Most computerized point-of-sale systems can be programmed to generate this information in as much detail as you want. Sales mix data provides the menu maker with the following information:

Popularity
Sales mix figures will show you the popularity of an item as it relates to other selections in its category. In the example above, the spinach dip sells twice as many orders as the nachos.

Price points

Sales mix data helps you identify how much the guests like to spend in each category. Our sample sales mix shows that sales of specific appetizer items decrease as their price increases. However, guests do not seem to make a distinction between $5.50 and $5.95. This helps you identify more profitable ways to structure your menu for enhanced guest appeal.

Preferences

The sales mix shows the types of foods that guests are choosing – poultry vs. beef or pastas over seafood. Trends can be easily discovered and used to create new menu items.

Planning

The sales mix also provides a way to estimate the sales of individual menu items based on projected daily sales. For example, let's say that past record-keeping indicates that 20% of your total food sales are represented by appetizer sales. Your food sales projection for the coming week is $30,000. You can safely project appetizer sales of about $6,000.

Your sales mix shows that Buffalo Wings comprise 30% of the dollar value of appetizer sales, so you can estimate $1800 in wing sales. At a price of $5.95, you now can project sales of 300 orders of Buffalo Wings next week, a great help when planning your purchases and scheduling prep staff.

Ron Yudd is an experienced speaker, trainer and consultant who helps operators design profit strategies and re-energize their passion for service. For more details and contact information, see Page 132.

29
Categorize Your Menu

There are two key decisions when laying out a menu – the presentation and the way the menu is categorized.

Presentation
The menu presentation is its style or format. It can be a postcard style (one panel), two-fold or three-fold menu. Size and format are usually driven by menu content (the number of items), style of the restaurant, concept and the frequency of menu revisions.

Categorization
To give the impression of value and variety (as it is perceived by the guest), the second most important element is how you categorize the items on the menu. Most restaurants' answer to the value/variety issue is to add items but this can lead to higher food costs, lower gross profits, higher labor costs, food waste and a diluted image/concept.

The importance of categorization
Categorization is simply the process of subdividing the menu into smaller, more specific categories. There are a number of advantages to doing this:

- The more the menu is categorized, the more the guest perceives variety.
- Women tend to read menus while men tend to scan theirs. Categorization makes either reading style more effective at bringing items to the guest's attention.

- The average time for a guest to make a menu decision is shortened to between 3-4 minutes (Postcard style was the quickest format). Categorizing helps the guest find what they want, leading to a quicker decision and ultimately a quicker table turn.
- Categorization allows you to merchandise those items (or categories) that you most want to sell.

Categorization tips

In creating categories on your menu, keep the following ideas in mind:

- Identify all categories on the menu.
- Place a minimum of 3-4, with a maximum of six items within a category. Any less and you lose variety/value in the category (and on the menu) – any more and the guests have to read too much.
- Place high-profit categories in the prime merchandising areas on the menu – the top two positions of the column or at the bottom of the column.

Categorizing your menu will make it easier for the guest to make a decision . . . and easier for them to decide to buy what you want to sell them.

Banger Smith is one of the recognized leaders in menu analysis and merchandising design who says he has never met a menu he couldn't make more profitable! For more details and contact information, see Page 131.

30
Menu Engineering

The average diner only spends 3½ minutes reading a menu and the smart operator makes the most of that time. Here are a few ways you can help your guests to buy what you want to sell, whether it is the house specialty or the most profitable item on the menu:

Highlighting

Since people's eyes roll across the page in a predictable path, any changes in the pattern catch their attention. For example, consider the placement of the word "special" to the immediate left of the menu item below.

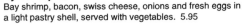

Bay Shrimp Quiche
Bay shrimp, bacon, swiss cheese, onions and fresh eggs in a light pastry shell, served with vegetables. 5.95

Special

Fish and Chips
A fillet of fresh cod or snapper deep fried in our popular beer batter, served with french fries. 6.95

Pacific Snapper Ragout
A fresh fillet sauteed in white wine and butter with olives, tomatoes and capers. 8.95

Lunch Top Sirloin
Freshly cut USDA choice, regular or teriyaki style, served with french fries. 8.95

The word "special" is not the key to this technique. The word could be "new" or "traditional" or any descriptive word which could accent a menu item. The key is that the word is placed asymmetrically – at a slight angle – and therefore catches the eye. Invariably, this will lead to an increase in the selection of the item by 10-20%.

Boxing

In many ways, boxing is the simplest and most powerful menu engineering tool to catch the eye of the diner. What is crucial here is to not dilute the effect of boxing by doing it too often. Two boxed patterns is the most that should be used on a page – one is better.

Dinner at Frank's Fish Farm

Dinner includes fresh chilled garden salad with your choice of home-style dressings and two kinds house-baked bread served with whipped honey butter and a medley of fresh seasonal vegetables

We proudly serve only the freshest varieties of fish from the waters of the Puget Sound and Alaska. We cook it to retain the full natural flavor and textures of the product. You have never had fish like this.

Deep Fried Calamari
Delicious rings of Monterey Bay Calamari deep fried, served with french fries and tartar sauce. 10.95

Seafood Cannelloni
Crepes stuffed with a delicious blend of fish, crab, shrimp mushrooms and onion in spicy tomato sauce. 10.95

Stuffed Mountain Trout Almondine
Fresh boneless rainbow trout brimming with crab and bay shrimp. 11.95

Baked Avocado and Shrimp Diablo
Two avocado halves with bay shrimp, mornay sauce and cheese. 12.50

Teriyaki Chicken Breast
A boneless breast of chicken marinated in teriyaki sauce and ginger. 11.50

Coquille di Mare
Crab, scallops and bay shrimp in a rich sauce with parmesan cheese. 12.95

Vegetarian Casserole
A medley of zucchini, eggplant, onions, tomatoes and peppers. 9.50

Crabtown Chicken
A tender chicken breast stuffed with crab, garlic butter and sherry sauce. 11.95

Shading

This technique is similar to boxing except for the type of outline used. Notice how the box in the figure on the following page has a dark band running horizontally (left to right) and vertically (right edge). By design, this band is slightly offset and the effect is three-dimensional. The menu item seems to be lifted off the page, which creates a disruption in the pattern the eye sees sweeping over the page. The eye stops briefly – and subconsciously considers the item. Menu items which are accented by the shading effect usually show a selection rate increase of at least 10%.

Dinner at Frank's Fish Farm

Dinner includes fresh chilled garden salad with your choice of home-style dressings and two kinds house-baked bread served with whipped honey butter and a medley of fresh seasonal vegetables.

We proudly serve only the freshest varieties of fish from the waters of the Puget Sound and Alaska. We cook it to retain the full natural flavor and textures of the product. You have never had fish like this.

Deep Fried Calamari
Delicious rings of Monterey Bay Calamari deep fried, served with french fries and tartar sauce. 10.95

Seafood Cannelloni
Crepes stuffed with a delicious blend of fish, crab, shrimp mushrooms and onion in spicy tomato sauce. 10.95

Stuffed Mountain Trout Almondine
Fresh boneless rainbow trout brimming with crab and bay shrimp. 11.95

Teriyaki Chicken Breast
A boneless breast of chicken marinated in teriyaki sauce and ginger. 11.50

Vegetarian Casserole
A medley of zucchini, eggplant, onions, tomatoes and peppers. 9.50

Baked Avocado and Shrimp Diablo
Two avocado halves with bay shrimp, mornay sauce and cheese. 12.50

Coquille di Mare
Crab, scallops and bay shrimp in a rich sauce with parmesan cheese. 12.95

Crabtown Chicken
A tender chicken breast stuffed with crab, garlic butter and sherry sauce. 11.95

Showcasing

This approach is an extension of the boxing/shading idea but it presents a package deal. For example, "a steak for two with a half bottle of Merlot." In the quick service segment, we would call this idea "bundling" but the effect would be the same.

The common thread is that the showcased section features a unique border, special graphic treatments or a pattern irregularity to attract the eye. Don't be surprised if sales of items showcased on your menu show immediate sales increases of 20% or more.

So let the menu offer a little theater . . . and sell more of your highest profit items as a result.

This material is excerpted from ***Menu Magic***™ by Bill Main, nationally-known author, consultant, speaker and Past President of the California Restaurant Association. For more details and contact information, see Page 128.

31
Signature Icons

This technique is the most direct – and least subtle – of the menu engineering techniques you might introduce on your menu. It is also the most fun and, predictably, the most effective. The concept is simple. Create a miniaturized version of your logo or similar graphic symbol that can be instantly tied to your establishment.

Place the icon slightly to the left of the menu item. This creates an interesting diversion for the eye as it scans the page. The icon subtlety suggests that the item is a "signature" – one that management obviously has given extra emphasis and attention – so it must be special, good or, at least, different.

Bay Shrimp Quiche
Bay shrimp, bacon, swiss cheese, onions and fresh eggs in a light pastry shell, served with vegetables. 5.95

Fish and Chips
A fillet of fresh cod or snapper deep fried in our popular beer batter, served with french fries. t6.95

Pacific Snapper Ragout
A fresh fillet sauteed in white wine and butter with olives, tomatoes and capers. 8.95

Lunch Top Sirloin
Freshly cut USDA choice, regular or teriyaki style, served with french fries. 8.95

This is how the subconscious mind of the restaurant patron works and it gives you the opportunity to use this fact in a way that enhances the dining experience while also selling those items which are most profitable.

Signature icons add style and texture to a menu, while offering a way to shift guest choices toward items that may be more seasonally advantageous. Let me clarify.

All menus have items which must be offered without regard to seasonal availability or cost factors. For example, during certain times of the year, lettuce is extremely expensive. But you can't stop serving salad because the price of lettuce is high, you simply absorb the extra cost and hope that lettuce prices drop soon. This is the point where the signature icon can help.

In the winter, when the price of lettuce is 40% above the summer level, you move the icon away from the Caesar Salad (popular in the summer and fall when lettuce prices are low and its profit is high) and place it next to the French Onion Soup (a lower cost item that is more appropriate for winter).

All you have done is to strategically use the icon to very subtly guide the guest to items that are more profitable for you at that point in time.

Be judicious in the use of icons, however. To maintain the appearance of "specialness," no more than one item in ten should receive this treatment. Signature icons – along with other techniques like highlighting, boxing, shading and showcasing – are the tools of pro-active menu engineering and menu profitability.

This material is excerpted from ***Menu Magic***™ by Bill Main, nationally-known author, consultant, speaker and Past President of the California Restaurant Association. For more details and contact information, see Page 128.

32
Page Positioning

The use of design principles – layout and graphic techniques, style and color concepts – to reshape and repackage your menu to sell those items that are inherently more profitable, is called menu engineering.

Defined, it is "the creative use of design and layout techniques to subtly and subconsciously influence the guest's selection behaviors." Its purpose is to sell those menu items that offer your guests the greatest value and which have the most favorable gross profit contribution.

A fascinating phenomenon about restaurant patrons' menu scanning behaviors is that their eye, as it scans the page, follows a predictable pattern. It is called page positioning or eye-gaze charting. The theory is simple. Whether a three-, two- or single-panel configuration, the eye flows across the page, following the predictable path illustrated below:

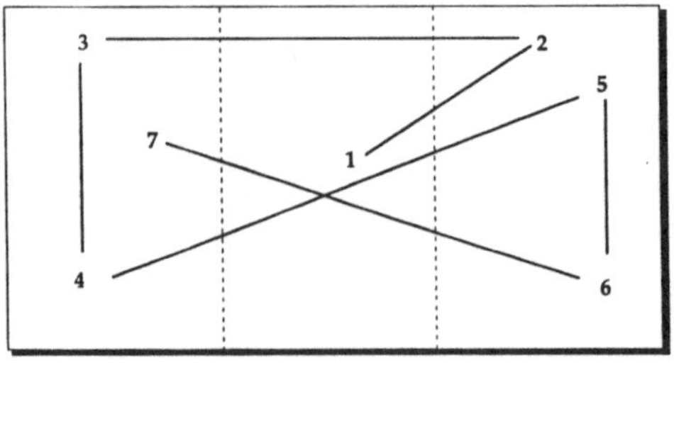

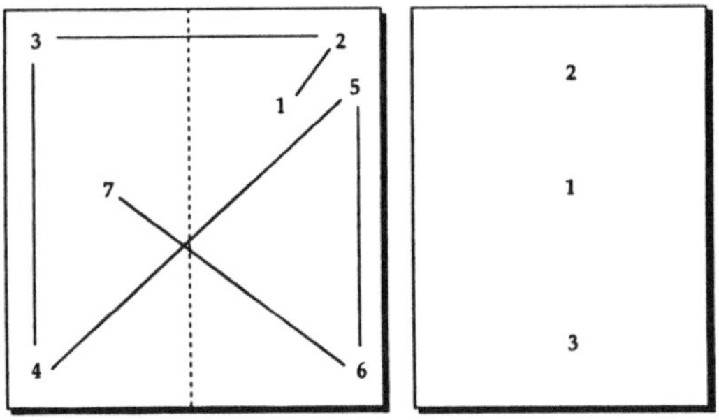

Take a look at your menu. Are the items that lie in the direct path of this eye gaze pattern those which provide the most favorable gross profit? Conversely, are the menu items in the least attractive location (#5,6,7) those which deliver the lowest gross profit contribution?

By understanding the concept of page positioning, you can start to create a layout that will maximize the profit potential of your menu.

This material is excerpted from ***Menu Magic™*** by Bill Main, nationally-known author, consultant, speaker and Past President of the California Restaurant Association. For more details and contact information, see Page 128.

33
Menu Item Placement

Have you discovered the secret advantages offered by strategic item placement? By highlighting your highest gross profit menu items, your menu will be more profitable.

First, your menu must be laid out by categories; (i.e., Appetizers, Soups and Salads, Seafood, Poultry, Side Dishes, Desserts and so forth.) Within these categories, look for a grouping of about 6-8 menu selections.

People do not read menus, they scan them. When they gaze across a page, their eyes follow a lazy, scanning path. When the eyes come across a category (such as starters), the subconscious reaction is to resist studying every item listed. As a result, the most frequently selected items are those in the first and last position in the category list, because these are the easiest for the reader's mind to grasp. It is as simple as that.

Therefore, the most obvious question is: does the first menu item in the category have the highest gross profit contribution? Does the last item listed have the second highest gross profit contribution? Are the rest of the menu selections arranged from the top-down and the bottom-up, to reflect a progressively lower gross profit contribution? Many operators miss the subtleties of item placement, either because they assume that patrons read every item on the menu or they simply arrange items in order of increasing price.

The idea of calculating gross profit contribution and then consciously arranging menu items in a category to take advantage of normal eye-gaze patterns sounds like techno-speak from academia. Not so – it is simple nuts and bolts menu analysis.

APPETIZERS		
Ceviche	5.95	← ***highest selection rate***
Escargot	4.50	
Clams	6.50	← ***lowest selection rate***
Shrimp	5.95	
Oysters on the Half Shell	6.50	← **highest selection rate**
ENTREES		
Blackened Red Snapper	13.50	← ***highest profit***
White Sea Bass	13.95	
Tiger Prawns	14.95	
Swordfish Pacifica	14.95	← ***lowest profit***
Chicken Breast Oskar	13.95	← ***lowest profit***
Sand Dabs Meuniere	12.95	
Dijon Saute	13.50	
Fettuccini Alfredo	12.95	← ***highest profit***

To take advantage of menu item placement strategy, you must have an accurate menu costing necessary so that you can calculate gross profit contribution. This can take some work but it is worth the effort.

You can easily improve the profitability of your menu simply by knowing how much gross profit each menu item contributes, understanding how patrons read the menu and how they make buying decisions . . . then arranging your menu items accordingly.

This material is excerpted from ***Menu Magic***™ by Bill Main, nationally-known author, consultant, speaker and Past President of the California Restaurant Association. For more details and contact information, see Page 128.

34
Value Perception Pricing

Menu prices should be based upon value perception of the guest – an intangible, often abstract combination of public perception and belief, shaped today by the print, audio and film media. At the core, it's often branded images. Excedrin vs. generic aspirin, Shell vs. the local independent, Oreo cookies vs. the house brand.

Setting price points must be based on value perception, never on a formula or derivative of raw cost. Patrons generally do not have a strong feeling about the raw cost of an item (even if they knew what it was).

But they do have a strong feeling about certain food product commodities. Take coffee, for instance. The going price for coffee is, let's say, $1.25. Your cost for giving a guest two cups of coffee (remember the free refill) along with sugar and cream might come to 20¢.

If your target food cost was 33% and you applied a standard pricing formula, you would sell coffee for 60¢. Why do you sell it for $1.25? Because you can get it! It is the market price, what guests expect to pay. It is the appropriate value-perceived price.

So the point of this example is obvious. Many chefs, kitchen managers and restaurant owners employ value perception pricing when it is obvious . . . then go back to formula pricing when it isn't. Every time they revert to the formula, they lose potential profit dollars.

There are three rules associated with setting price points by value perception pricing:

- Do not make pricing decisions in a vacuum. Shop the competition within a five-mile radius and/or fifteen minute drive time of your operation. Research – and learn – competitors' portion sizes, quality level, cooking style, plate presentation and price points. Use this data to see how restaurant guests perceive value and decide if your price point is fair and equitable.

- Do not let chefs or kitchen managers price a menu by themselves. They are the furthest from the guest and, therefore, have less feel for market conditions relative to perceived value. They are supply-driven in that they are responsible for creating, producing and delivering the product. They are best informed about creative and production issues, not market conditions.

- Talk to your service staff – they are closest to your patrons and know more about value perception pricing than 1000 surveys! They are demand-driven in that their job is to sell the product, so they have a different sense of connection with the menu. Formalize and systemize the gathering of opinions from servers by utilizing a server focus group at least once a quarter.

These items are the critical input you need to establish price points that will maximize your sales and profits. Sell value, not just the product.

This material is excerpted from ***Menu Magic***™ by Bill Main, nationally-known author, consultant, speaker and Past President of the California Restaurant Association. For more details and contact information, see Page 128.

35
Rounding Strategy

This concept is so simple it is almost embarrassing to talk about, yet few operators seem to understand its potential for increasing profitability.

When a restaurant sets menu prices by applying a formula, you see odd prices ($7.35, $10.15) or prices set in increments of 25¢ ($8.25, $9.75). This is an inherently wrong – and expensive – pricing approach.

Value perception pricing dictates that for all menu items above $5.00, the guest does not recognize price points other than $0.50 and $0.95 – could care less, in fact. The practical reality is that people do not read menus. In their quick, subconscious "read" on price, they only really see the 11 in $11.95 or the 8 in $8.95. There may be some merit to the $0.50 mid-dollar point, although it dissipates quickly in the mind of the guest once you break the $10.00 barrier.

For menu items priced under $5.00, the waters are a bit more muddy, because the significance of a dime (10¢) or a quarter (25¢) is much greater. As a general rule, menu items with price points set at levels of .25, .50, .75 and .95 seem to be agreeable. In other words, if you can charge $3.15 for sausage and eggs, you can probably charge $3.25 without any resistance.

A simple illustration should clarify the point:

Assume a menu item has been selling for $14.25 and you sell 25 per day. That translates to 9,000+ sold per year. Using the rounding strategy, if you can charge $14.50 instead of the current price of $14.25 without the market even noticing, you have just given yourself a "gift of profit" in the amount of nearly $2,300!

In my experience, once an operator grasps this simple pricing philosophy, their profit potential will increase by at least 2-3%.

This material is excerpted from ***Menu Magic***™ by Bill Main, nationally-known author, consultant, speaker and Past President of the California Restaurant Association. For more details and contact information, see Page 128.

Part 4

Points to Ponder

36
Find a Signature Item and Grow for It

This is the story of how a simple Chinese Chicken Salad accompanied by freshly baked zucchini bread built a restaurant, a banquet business and became the famous Dianne Salad of Pasadena.

The tale started in 1978 at the Greenstreet Restaurant in Pasadena, California when Dianne, a friend of the owners, developed a knockout dressing for Chinese Chicken Salad. When they introduced the salad, everyone at the restaurant fell in love with it and shared their excitement with other guests.

The popularity of this item grew with the ladies at lunch and the businessmen watching their waistlines. The new star was christened the Dianne Salad and added freshly baked zucchini bread to the dining experience.

The press got wind of the salad from Greenstreet's fans and the subsequent stories increased the salad's following and reputation. As a result of the exposure generated by the Dianne Salad, Greenstreet was voted the best lunch restaurant in a popularity poll.

In 1992, the restaurant added a pick-up window so that Dianne Salad addicts could quickly satisfy their habits. As the convenience grew so did the large orders and soon the Dianne became a party favorite. The offering grew from plated luncheons to party bags to cartons to feed 200 on 30 minutes notice!

In 1996, they revised the menu, adding all new salads and the Dianne Salad (in two sizes) is proudly and prominently displayed in a boxed center section. They also created a new combination – New York Steak and Dianne Salad – which placed the salad in a starring role on the dinner menu.

By popular demand, Greenstreet recently added a full banquet facility to provide a new place for the Dianne Salad and its friends to party!

How much salad do they sell? Weekly production exceeds 800 lb. of poached and pulled chicken, 125 lb. of warm toasted almonds, 50 cases of lettuce to be finely shredded, a truck full of mai fun noodles and cases of fresh oranges for the garnish. This is all in addition to endless batches of secret dressing that is "just light enough, sweet enough and tangy enough."

So what does all this mean? They calculated that the Dianne Salad, directly or indirectly, is responsible for 30% of the restaurant's total sales! The next goal is to take the Dianne Salad, the secret dressing and the zucchini bread into retail production.

This shows what can be done with a signature salad. What is your restaurant famous for? What are you going do with it?

Phyllis Ann Marshall and her company, FoodPower, help restaurants mine the gold hidden in their menus. She specializes in merchandising with food and menus. For more details and contact information, see Page 129.

37
Menu Delights

Everyone talks about the importance of satisfying your guests, but in today's competitive market, satisfaction will not be enough to keep you growing and prospering over the long term. As the foodservice pie gets sliced into more and more pieces, it is important to go beyond mere satisfaction and become memorable in the eyes of your guests.

To be memorable, we must not only ***meet*** our guests' expectations, we must ***exceed*** them. In other words, we must make sure our guests are ***delighted!*** Here are a few delightful things you can do with menus to make yourself more memorable:

Menu presentation

Your menu can be something to talk about. The "talking power" could be in the physical nature of the menu itself or in the way it is presented to the guest. Menus on gold pans, bottles, paddles or boards were once the rage and might make a comeback in themed operations. The menu at Mike Hurst's 15th Street Fisheries in Ft. Lauderdale, Florida is a framed presentation set on an easel by the side of the table.

Range of items

You could make a point of difference based on the range of items you offer. For example, if you had a large menu, you might say, "The great thing about a big menu is that everyone can always find something they like." If you had a small menu, you could say, "We only have ten items on our menu because we think a restaurant can only do a credible job with about six items. If a place has a huge menu, you know many of them have to be filler." Who is right? It depends on whether you have a large menu or a small menu!

Braille menus

If a guest spoke another language, you would try to get someone who could translate, wouldn't you? Why not extend the same courtesy to deaf or blind guests? Most towns have a local agency who provides services for the blind. Ask them to translate your menu to Braille.

Menus on tape

A blind friend told me that only about 10% of blind people can read Braille. A seminar attendee had a wonderful idea – she had her entire menu recorded on a walkman-type recorder and offered it to blind diners. This way they could go through the menu at their own pace and still get the descriptions of the menu items.

Menus in foreign languages

You would never offer English-speaking guests a menu written in Chinese, yet you think nothing of presenting a menu written in English to a Chinese-speaking guest. It is only courteous to offer menus that guests can understand. Ask your multilingual "regulars" to help you translate your menu into other languages. Include English subtitles for your staff. This is a small gesture of respect for a small segment of your market, but it will clearly reflect your passion for diner delight.

This material was adapted from a list of more than 200 delightful practices in the book ***Guest-Based Marketing*** by Bill Marvin, The Restaurant Doctor. For more details and contact information, see Page 130.

38

Don't Forget the Side Dishes

Side dish sales offer the opportunity to create an upsell situation, adding anywhere from \$1.50 to \$3.50 to the check average by merchandising vegetable and starch items (traditionally considered to be plate "fillers") as sexy and interesting "must try" items in themselves.

Providing a selection of a la carte side dishes on your menu allows entree prices to be kept lower. Selling one or more side dishes can bring the average check back up to a level that can produce a satisfactory gross profit contribution.

Historically, side dishes are dish-up items, able to be reconstituted, or reheated to order from a steam table, pantry or sauté line. An interesting selection of side dishes on the menu allows the guest ordering the Porterhouse steak to exchange a baked Idaho potato for garlic mashed potatoes or to substitute wild rice for al dente vegetables to go with the poached salmon. It lets them add an order of creamed corn Parmesan or spinach anisette just for the fun of it or to share the experience of new flavors with others at the table.

Side dishes also present a great opportunity for patrons to share an item or order one or two extra items "for the table." This practice is gaining favor in casual and fine dining restaurants in all parts of the country. After all, we have been doing this with Chinese food all these years – what's the difference?

Side dishes have a minimal impact on the line setup in the kitchen because they are prepped in advance and feature a minimum of hands-on fabrication. Most side dishes accompany a main course, allowing maximum range of experimentation by new or regular customers.

In the words of "Coach" Don Smith, "The answer is yes. What's the question?" The days of "no substitutions" are virtually gone. So think of side dishes as an incredible marketing and merchandising tool that can inject some real fun, interest, diversity and "wow" into your menu with a minimum investment in research and development.

Side dishes do not have to be complicated to be memorable. Take a #10 can of high quality sweet corn, add some cream, a few spices and a sprinkle of freshly grated Parmesan cheese. Put it under the cheese melted for 30 seconds and bingo – an unusual item with fabulous flavor that costs less than 60¢ and can sell for $1.95 . . . maybe even $2.50 or $2.95.

In the language of your customers, this one is a "no-brainer!"

This material is excerpted from ***Menu Magic***™ by Bill Main, nationally-known author, consultant, speaker and Past President of the California Restaurant Association. For more details and contact information, see Page 128.

39
Fatal Flaws in Menu Design

What you see is what you get in menus. If the menu is exciting and interesting, the evening will have more promise. If the menu creates problems for diners, they will be more apprehensive. Here are a few of the more common fatal flaws in menu design.

Menu print too small to read easily

Guests cannot order what they cannot read. This is a particular annoyance for older diners who dislike reminders that their eyes are less sharp. If your menu is hard to read, either raise the lighting level or use larger type. Often, changing the paper or ink colors will improve contrast and make the menu more readable. Watch your guests as they read your menu, be alert for signs of difficulty and take any necessary action.

Menus that are too big to handle easily

Menus make a statement – just be careful what you're saying. Menu size has a relationship to the amount of information you want to present and the size of your tables. It is awkward for your guests if the menu is too large to set down on the table. You must usually make large menus of a heavier material to prevent them from folding – make sure they do not get too heavy for the guest to handle.

No English translations

Formality is one thing, snobbishness is another. When a restaurant does not print the menu in the native language of their guests, it is pretentious and rude.

Even if you just explain the items in subtitles, it is just common courtesy to have a menu your English-speaking guests can read.

Antiquated menu presentations

If your menu looks like 1950 and your restaurant doesn't, you may have a problem. Outdated menus can lead to an image that you are an outmoded restaurant. I'm not suggesting you should change the items on your menu, just look at how you are presenting them. Often a fresh look can give your operation a boost in the market.

No daily special insert

Everything you do in the restaurant must reflect your concern for guest gratification, attention to detail and professionalism. An incomplete menu is an annoyance for your guests and the staff who have to correct the error. If your menu should have a sheet with the day's specials on it, coach your greeters to check each menu to be sure the inserts are in place. Consider changing the color of the menu inserts each day to make it easier to spot outdated ones.

Entrees that don't look like their photos

Full color photographs can be an effective way to market your entrees. Photographs create expectations in your guests and entice them to order. However, if the item you serve does not live up to the advance billing, you will not have met your guests' expectations and they will be disappointed, no matter how good the item turns out to be.

This material was adapted from the book, ***Restaurant Basics: Why Guests Don't Come Back and What You Can Do About It,*** by Bill Marvin, The Restaurant Doctor. For more details and contact information, see Page 130.

40
Profitable Pointers

The discussion of how to build more profitable menus can be endless . . . and you still have a restaurant to run. So here are a few short – but profitable – ideas that have not yet been addressed:

Increase "add-on" sales

Although we look at the menu as the most important marketing tool, the supporting cast of merchandising pieces is vital to increasing "add-on" sales per guest.

- We know that when you add the wine list to the menu you increase wine sales.
- We know that when you offer a special sheet at the table, you increase sales of specialty items.
- We know that when you offer a dessert menu to the table, you increase dessert sales.

Combine your merchandising program with a well-trained service staff and watch sales and profits soar!

Talk healthy, eat tasty

After analyzing sales mix reports from roughly 50 different restaurants, it appears that while guests are talking healthy, they are eating tasty. People tend to eat healthier at home and "splurge" in restaurants. While no food is actually ***un***healthy, here are a few things to consider about merchandising items with lower fat/cholesterol/sodium on your menu:

- Focus groups tell us that guests want to see healthy options on the menu. However, they are usually "good for those who are looking for them, but not me."
- The mix of "healthy" entrees should be no more than 1%-7% of the total entree mix.
- Highlighting lower fat items (with a heart or other icon denoting a "healthy" option) in a menu category may actually have a negative impact on that item's sales. Put heart-healthy items in a separate category rather than interspersing them with your other offerings.

When to drop an item

A general rule of thumb is that you should consider dropping an item from the menu when it accounts for less than 3% of the sales in its category. (Of course, if you have several items that are selling at 3% of the category, then the choice is not automatic.) Items that sell less than 3% seldom justify their potential liability in terms of wasted labor, poor quality and spoilage.

Be wary of single use ingredients

Another key to a more profitable menu is to minimize the number of inventory items that must be carried to produce it. This reduces purchasing time, storage requirements and spoilage. One reason that Chinese and Mexican restaurants are so profitable is that they use a minimal number of ingredients to produce a maximum number of menu items. Be wary of specialty ingredients that are only used in one item, unless that item is a signature of the restaurant. If this is the case, look for other ways to use that ingredient.

Banger Smith is one of the recognized leaders in menu analysis and merchandising design who says he has never met a menu he couldn't make more profitable! For more details and contact information, see Page 131.

41
Heart-Healthy is Happening

People may talk healthy and eat tasty when they go out, but paying more attention to the nutritional content of your menu may just be the direction of the future. All things being equal, I believe many diners would prefer to eat healthier food – they are just unwilling to change their diets in order to do it!

This suggests that you may be able to sell heart-healthy (lower fat, cholesterol and sodium) versions of your patrons' traditional menu choices ***provided*** the heart-healthy versions taste terrific! There may be a real opportunity to gain a controlling position in the market by building a reputation as a great restaurant that also happens to accommodate heart-healthy dining.

With the right recipes, raw ingredients and equipment, you can prepare heart-healthy dishes that are every bit as tasty as any conventional offering. Of course, not all selections have low fat versions but I have designed a well-balanced restaurant menu where 75% of the items meet the American Heart Association standards for heart-healthy dining . . . including hamburgers and french fries!

(For the sake of reference, I used naturally low fat beef that had fewer calories than chicken and about the same fat level as fish. The fries were a quality potato that was cooked in hot air rather than deep fried – and actually tasted like potatoes!)

Here is another example of how you can accommodate heart-healthy dining without going crazy: Mike Nemeth owns a legendary Mexican restaurant in Colorado Springs. After noticing that his guests were becoming more nutritionally conscious, he decided to offer a chimichanga (usually a deep-fried burrito) that is crisped in the oven rather than in a fryer. It tastes as good as (or better than) the fried version without the added fat. Because he makes it a point to tell his guests what he is doing, he uses the item to develop word-of-mouth and grow his sales as diners pass the word to others.

It is not always that easy, however, and it often takes some experimentation to modify menus to lower the fat, cholesterol and sodium without losing taste. But you can do it if it is important enough to you. With the nutritional content of restaurant food under suspicion, three or four healthy choices on your menu can help you become the restaurant of choice with your patrons who are concerned about what they eat.

It may come as a surprise, but one group that is becoming particularly worried about nutrition is long haul truck drivers. As a result, you are likely to find a wider range of heart-healthy menu choices at a truck stop than in most American restaurants! How's that for challenging the stereotype?

If you want more information on the subject, contact your local chapter of the American Heart Association.

This material was adapted from ***Guest-Based Marketing*** and ***Restaurant Basics: Why Guests Don't Come Back and What You Can Do About It,*** by Bill Marvin, The Restaurant Doctor. For more details and contact information, see Page 130.

42
Think Small

Piatti Piccolo. Tapas. Appetizers. Half portions. Small plates. Whatever you call them, they are a tremendous way to build business and enhance satisfaction. But won't smaller portions mean smaller check averages? You will give up sales, won't you?

Well, maybe yes . . . and maybe no. Some high-ticket operators may yield a bit on the check average, but increased guest counts and greater frequency of regular users will more than make up any difference! Here are some thoughts to ponder:

- Look at the year-end summary of openings and closings in ***Nation's Restaurant News*** and you will notice that those super-pricey, extra-special occasion restaurants bite the dust more often than their lower-priced counterparts. People like to splurge once in awhile but they just can't afford to do it very often. This does not necessarily mean that people will be satisfied with lesser quality.

- You can't take percentages to the bank and the same holds true of check averages. One hundred guests at $35.00 each will put more cash in your pocket than 50 guests at $50.00. By giving patrons greater choice in the overall cost of their evening, you increase the potential for return visits.

- It is hard to keep an all-star restaurant staff happy and fully employed if you are only busy one or two nights a week. Wouldn't they be happier (and stay longer) if business was at or near capacity 4-5 nights a week instead?

- How about kids? Today's children are tomorrow's regulars and you want them to develop a taste for the better things in life (like your restaurant!) Few parents will order the kids a full rack of ribs but a four-rib order might be an easy sell. If Mom or Dad order it themselves, so much the better. If they can't get it from you, they'll go somewhere where they can!

- Many of the new, interesting, and unique food items on today's menus can be intimidating. Guests who would be reluctant to order an unfamiliar entree at $17.00 might take a chance on it at $8.00 or $9.00. They can even pass it around and give everyone at the table a taste without breaking the bank.

- Guests can get so excited about your menu items that they just can't decide. Give them the option of ordering an assortment of appetizers or half-orders so they can get a better understanding of your style and quality level. Their check average is often higher than guests eating traditional meals at neighboring tables and they are likely to come back more often.

- Smaller portions may even help you fill your seats on a Tuesday or Wednesday evening, because guests will know they can go out midweek and still afford to dine out on the weekend!

The adage that "more is better" does not always hold true when it comes to menu portions. Think small and you can make big bucks!

Howard Cutson is Principal of Cutson Associates, a customer service-focused consulting firm specializing in bar operations and creative service training. For more details and contact information, see Page 124.

43
Paint Them a Picture

If your menu items are not appropriately described or if the description requires the server to spend time restating things that the guests can (or should be) able to read clearly, you are causing your guests more work and wasting your servers' time.

Most menu descriptions are boring or at the least, predictable. To illustrate what powerful pictures you can paint with the right words, consider the following description from the J. Peterman clothing catalog and compare it to the typical descriptions from other mail order merchants:

> ***You've been away from his studio only an hour; already you want to go back. Winter sunlight coming through unshuttered windows, oranges on a table, fish in a bowl, you reclining voluptuously inside the framework of a teak opium bed. What makes it complete is Matisse himself. He studies the effect of your upper and lower leg inside your pants. He paints the suggestion of curves and physical warmth on a blank canvas. His eyes travel to you, back to the canvas, back to you. Hours pass. You've never felt more closely observed, more at ease.***

Now you may not have room for descriptions of this length on your menu (. . . or do you?) but perhaps you could learn from the way J. Peterman presents their products and take some of the dullness out of your menu copy. Let's consider a typical menu description like the following for a basic hamburger:

A third-pound of ground beef, charbroiled to perfection. Served with lettuce and tomato.

Is any picture being painted? What does "charbroiled to perfection" really mean, anyway? Now let's try it another way:

This is the classic hamburger – simple yet so seldom found. A full third-pound of freshly-ground lean beef, pungent and sizzling from the charbroiler, framed with crisp lettuce and that one perfect slice of vine-ripened tomato.

Does this sound a little more interesting? Might your staff have more to talk to your guests about? Could you even charge a premium for such a "classic?"

The point is that dining is a total sensory experience – sight, sound, taste and smell – and the savvy operator will appeal to them all. Perhaps you can persuade a creative writer to design your menu script for you or perhaps there is a member of your staff with talent as a wordsmith. However you do it, use your menu copy to paint a word picture that really says something to your patrons.

Be careful not to promise anything that you do not actually deliver – truth in menu is alive and well! Still, creating sensuality in your descriptions will enhance your guests' experience and give your staff more time to promote the products you really want to sell.

Raymond Goodman is a Professor at the University of New Hampshire and the leading authority on dining room management and service management consulting. For more details and contact information, see Page 126.

44
Branding

Branding is the sleeping giant of opportunity. Including branded products on your menu is the very definition of value-added thinking and value-perception pricing. Brand identity is here to stay and, depending on the specific menu application, it can be extremely effective for increasing both the range and diversity of the food items you offer.

More important, the right branded products create instant credibility about product quality. The perceived quality of the branded product, so promoted in the mainstream media, becomes the quality of the operator by association.

Research suggests that four out of five diners believe a restaurant's image is enhanced by the use of branded products and that these diners are willing to pay more for products containing ingredients whose quality they recognize and appreciate.

For example, Prawns Sauté at $15.50, becomes Prawns Dijonaise just by adding Grey Poupon Dijon Mustard at the finish. The new price is $17.95 and when I made this change in my own restaurant, sales increased more than 20%. $2.45 is a decent return on 31¢ worth of mustard, wouldn't you say?

When the Dreyers/Edy's Grand Ice Cream logo was added to the dessert section of a popular West Coast family restaurant's menu, the operator added 50¢ to each item and dessert sales increased by more than 20%! The guest subconsciously saw the 30-second TV spot in which the Dreyer's/Edy's quality was reinforced in glossy, vivid color . . . and the flow-through profit is approximately 30¢ extra on each dessert sold, reflecting the premium cost base.

Branding must be done selectively and with caution. Menus should be accented by branded products, not driven by them. As a rule, 1-2% of the menu items should feature a branded identity or reference.

Remember that guests don't read menus and that merchandising, design and layout concepts ultimately drive profitability. If they are not going to read menus, leverage their selection behaviors by adding recognized product brands to the menu . . . and keep the profits!

This material is excerpted from ***Menu Magic***™ by Bill Main, nationally-known author, consultant, speaker and Past President of the California Restaurant Association. For more details and contact information, see Page 128.

45
Picture This!

A picture is worth a thousand words . . . and a picture of a menu item (or seeing the actual item itself) can be worth thousands of dollars in sales! Most people love to see what they're going to get, or what they're missing out on. Imagine a catalog – for clothes, garden tools, toys or furniture – without pictures. Unthinkable!

Appeal to all the senses
This in not to suggest you should turn your menu into a clone of Denny's (although the heavy photo content certainly works well for them) but guests buy more with their eyes, their noses and their tastebuds, and less from reading a list of menu items.

If you have ever seen your guests' reactions as a server walked across the dining room with a huge strawberry shortcake or a steaming order of garlic-infused shrimp de jhonge, you understand why peoples' mouths start watering when they see, smell or taste great food. This is the opportunity that you can exploit to create a more powerful menu presentation.

Using pictures to sell
If you aren't ready to put pictures on your menu, start by at least using photos in the kitchen so the cooks know how each menu item should look. Have the same photo over the slide so the servers can exercise some quality control in the kitchen and use the same pictures in training manuals and recipe books.

Repetition is the key to memory and consistency and when a bartender or server can mentally picture the item, they will be more likely to describe it to the guest in a highly visual way.

A picture in three dimensions is even better. When a guest can actually see the food on a display stand, tray or cart, they are more likely to buy. Just look at the increasing popularity of food displays, lobster tanks, sampling, tableside preparations, dessert trays and cigar boxes and you will understand the direction in which this trend is moving.

Anything you can do to allow your guests see, smell, hear, touch or taste before buying will cause them to walk away delighted, having ordered and received exactly what they wanted!

Picture that!

Peter Good has spent the better part of 25 years in the hospitality industry. His book, ***The Magic of Hospitality,*** captures real-life customer service experiences. For more details and contact information, see Page 125.

46
Stupid Menu Tricks

A featured segment of the old David Letterman Show offered "Stupid Pet Tricks" – strange things that people taught their pets to do. I suppose they made sense to the pet owner, but they were a joke to the audience. There must be a similar mind set in some operators. Here are some of the more common "stupid menu tricks" – practices that must make sense to someone in management, but which are a joke to the guests:

Printed menus with handwritten changes

Image is everything and handwritten changes on a printed menu does not look professional. If you make a change (including the vintage year of a wine), print a new menu. Desktop publishing and cafe style menus makes in-house changes easier than ever. If you like ease of change and want color, print four color menu shells and overprint the details on the computer.

Specials board showing yesterday's offerings

Promoting expired specials suggests that you are not paying attention. Make it a routine responsibility after the meal to erase the special from the board. It is part of shifting your perspective to see everything in the restaurant from your guest's point of view.

Illegible blackboard specials

Using a blackboard to list specials can be an effective marketing aid . . . but only if your guests can read what is on the board! Be sure the person writing your daily specials has a neat, easily readable hand.

Recitation of specials that goes on . . . and on

Limit verbal presentations of daily specials to two items, three at the outside. Your guests can't remember any more information anyway. More choices wastes the server's time and makes the diner impatient. How about a mini menu explaining the day's specials that you leave on the table after the verbal presentation? This way your guests won't have to feel uncomfortable because they can't remember what you said.

Misspelled or grammatically incorrect menu copy

Menu writing is more than simply listing your entrees. Verify the spelling of entries with a culinary dictionary and carefully proofread the final copy.

Soiled or wrinkled menus or table tents

Greasy, dog-eared or sticky menus with creases, stains or beverage rings get the meal off to a bad start. The condition of your menus can cause patrons to draw conclusions about the cleanliness of your kitchen. If that conclusion is unfavorable, everything you do will be suspect. Inspect all menus before the meal and throw out all those that are not perfect.

Listing items guests can't order at the time

It is annoying if your guests have to consult their watch when reading your menu. When it is noon and the menu lists items that are not available after 11:30 or items that are not available until 5:00, you lose points. Be sure your menu tells your guests what you ***can*** do for them, not what you ***can't!*** I applaud the desire to save money on printing, but at what cost?

This material was adapted from the book, ***Restaurant Basics: Why Guests Don't Come Back and What You Can Do About It,*** by Bill Marvin, The Restaurant Doctor. For more details and contact information, see Page 130.

47
"Tonight we are featuring..."

For many people, the daily "special" is anything but special. Specials are often presumed to be leftovers or the result of some screw up in the kitchen that the house must get rid of quickly.

An effective way to change the impression of your daily "off the menu" items is to refer to them as your "featured" dishes. Train your servers to announce "tonight we are featuring . . ." This simple shift can enhance their ability to promote the dishes and increase the sale of certain menu items. "Featured items" can give you a subtle, but crucial, point of difference from your competition.

Here are a few reasons why it is to your advantage to offer one or two "featured items" at every meal:

Your guests will like them
"Featured items" help prevent regulars from getting bored with the menu.

You can challenge and involve your staff
Ask your crew to help you create featured items that are unique, interesting and that your guests will love.

You can feature low-cost dishes
For example, when I was a student, a local restaurant featured all-you-can-eat spaghetti every Monday night. They were always packed and sold mass quantities of beer (at full price!)

You can take the load off the kitchen

If you have days or meal periods you know will be extremely busy (like Mother's Day), feature items that require minimal final preparation in the kitchen. Fewer labor-intensive dishes will reduce waiting times and increase table turns.

You can develop a local identity

Locals and visitors alike appreciate "home grown" favorites. In many cases your cost of ingredients will be lower or you may be able to charge a premium price for something a little different, not to mention the nostalgia value of an item that someone's grand-mother used to make years ago.

You can capitalize on seasonal prices

Fresh strawberries are an excellent example of a product with dramatic price swings depending on seasonal availability. Featuring strawberry pie and strawberry daiquiris "in season" means lower cost and higher quality products.

A consistent focus on featured dishes can be a double win in any restaurant. Guests have the option of trying new and interesting dishes while you have another means of involving your staff, improving kitchen efficiency and boosting your profit margins.

Jim Laube, CPA, is President of the Center for Foodservice Education and a consultant in profitability and financial management. For more details and contact information, see Page 127.

48
Burn the Menus!

What would happen to food and beverage sales in your operation if all your menus suddenly went up in smoke? Could your servers, bartenders, hosts and hostesses, receptionists, and managers describe all your soups, salads, appetizers, entrees and desserts from memory? Would they know portion sizes, prices, ingredients and preparation methods without a menu?

How much do they know?

- New servers are usually tested on menu items during their initial training but after awhile, they probably forget details of less popular items or items offered on shifts they don't usually work unless they refer to a menu.

- Bartenders often know little about a menu, since all they usually have to do is take an order for an appetizer, a meal at the bar or perhaps refer the guest to a server.

- Telephone receptionists are always fielding questions from guests yet they can rarely respond to all those queries competently without referring to a menu.

- Many greeters have to go the menu to answer basic questions. Even managers often have to get a cook or a server (or grab a menu) to answer a guest's question.

This is not always the case, of course, but if you cannot effectively present your offerings to guests without referring to the menu itself, what message does that send about how important your food is to you?

A suggestion

Hold a quarterly contest for all servers, bartenders, cooks, hosts and managers. The goal is to memorize the menu – items, ingredients, portion sizes, prices and methods of preparation. The person from each skill position who does the best wins something of value (a gift certificate, days off, reserved parking or whatever) and enters the finals. Grand prizes should be substantial (a TV, a trip or whatever you can trade for.)

A contest creates healthy competition and is a great learning activity. Confidence will increase (service always improves with increased confidence) and smiles will replace looks of fear when guests ask questions. You will likely hear your staff suggesting appetizers, recommending entrees and raving about desserts – all without referring to a menu.

A printed menu is one way to introduce guests to your food offerings but it should not be a crutch. The same job can also be done verbally, often more effectively. When your staff becomes personally involved with the menu it is a win-win experience for everyone. There are higher sales for house and improved tips for the staff, of course, but the guests are the biggest winners – they are likely to find ready answers to their questions, have a better time and enjoy much more personal service.

When you can burn the menus and still deliver your message effectively, everybody wins!

Peter Good has spent the better part of 25 years in the hospitality industry. His book, ***The Magic of Hospitality,*** captures real-life customer service experiences. For more details and contact information, see Page 125.

49
Tell Your Quality Story

Let me tell you a story about telling stories:

I was in Northern California to consult for a high volume restaurant. I arrived early the day before I was to begin because I wanted to have dinner and "shop" the restaurant anonymously before I came in contact with any of the managers or staff. It turned out to be one of the best culinary experiences I had encountered in quite some time. The entire meal was absolutely delicious. From appetizer to dessert, everything was creatively prepared, fresh and perfectly cooked.

When I met with the owner the next morning, I told him how impressed I was with my dinner the night before. With obvious pride, he explained to me many of the steps and details his chef and kitchen personnel go through to serve the best possible food, like making everything from scratch, including all of the dressings, breads and desserts.

He told me about the slow roasting of the Prime Rib and how they prepare all their salad ingredients daily, never using pre-made or canned items. He made the point that they grind their own gourmet coffee beans fresh for each pot and buy most of their fish right off the docks the same morning that it is caught.

I was unaware of any of these details because my server had not mentioned them and I had not noticed any of this information on the menu. I asked him how many of his guests he thought were aware of all the little things the restaurant did to make their dining experience the best it can possibly be. His reply was timid. "I don't know, probably not too many," he said.

As we talked, he became convinced that, at the least, he had to tell his restaurant's quality story on the back page of the menu – to let his guests know the care and attention to quality that goes into every meal the restaurant serves.

So he added the additional menu copy and now he finds that many, if not most of his guests notice and read the back page of the menu. Beside receiving many positive comments (which always feels good), telling their quality story has given the restaurant an important point of difference from their competitors.

(Did I mention that right after he changed the menu, his sales "magically" increased by 10%? Was adding the story responsible for the additional volume? Who knows? . . . but it sure didn't hurt!)

Raising your guests' awareness enhances their level of expectation and increases the perceived value of the entire dining experience. What is your story? Are you telling it? If you don't, who will?

Jim Laube, CPA, is President of the Center for Foodservice Education and a consultant in profitability and financial management. For more details and contact information, see Page 127.

50
More Stupid Menu Tricks

Sometimes the stupid mistakes in menu structure are those created by policy rather than by design. Your goal is to lead your guests to select the items you want them to order, not to irritate them. Here are several decidedly guest-unfriendly practices to avoid:

Only dinner-sized portions at lunch

Most Americans still eat their larger meal in the evening. They are conditioned to accept larger portions (and the accompanying higher prices) later in the day. Failure to offer more traditional luncheon-size portions at midday effectively makes the menu unworkable. The guest is in a no-win situation. They must either order something they don't really want or get up and leave.

Charging 50¢ extra for blue cheese dressing

I know that blue cheese dressing costs a little more than the average. I also know that some dressings cost a little less than the average. To keep from confusing (and annoying) your guests, base your prices on the average and keep it simple. If you want to tip the scales a bit, develop a tasty, low-cost house dressing and feature that as a signature item.

Fixed price menus with surcharges for anything (except perhaps caviar)

If you advertise a fixed price menu, that is what your guests expect. If your "fixed price" menu becomes like buying a car with all the added extras, you will be remembered as fondly as the typical car salesman! Fixed price menus can be attractive to diners – just don't run the risk of making your guests feel cheated by trying to run the tab up on them.

Menus that completely change every day

A totally fluid menu can confuse your market about what to expect from your restaurant. This general idea has worked in some small restaurants but the danger is still there. If you think this style has some promise for you, consider a weekly menu instead. Perhaps two or three solid signature items backed up with two specials can satisfy your need for a limited menu without becoming confusing for your guests.

Failure to offer non-meat options

There are a growing number of people in the country who choose to reduce or eliminate their meat consumption. Additionally, many more are watching their fat and cholesterol intake and find non-meat entrees a more frequent menu choice. By reflecting this preference on your menu, you become a viable destination for these diners. An added advantage of meatless entrees is that your profit margins are often more attractive.

Too many (or too few) items on the menu

An enjoyable and effortless dining experience creates the good time your guests want. Logic says that the more choices you give a guest, the more likely they are to get exactly what they want. This could be true, but the process of making all the choices can be cruel and unusual punishment! Guests do not come to your restaurant to become students of your menu. They should be able to find a choice that interests them within a reasonable period of time.

Giving people unlimited choices does not enhance their dining experience. In fact, it may only allow them to eat what they would eat at home and restaurants ought to be more special than that. Offering a unique house dressing, a signature soup or a distinctive side dish (rather than an endless array of choices) is easier on the kitchen, faster for the service staff and more interesting for the guest. See that your menu offers enough variety to give guests a reasonable choice but not so many items that it is confusing.

No signature items on the menu

Signature items are those menu offerings for which you are (or would like to be) famous. If you do not have signature items, what is there to separate you from all your competitors in the minds of your market? If you have special items that nobody else can match, you have a competitive advantage. So what are you going to be famous for? What are your guests going to tell their friends about?

Signature items help you create an image in people's minds and help them remember you when they make the dining decision. Signature items do not have to be your most expensive menu offering. They do not even have to relate to your main menu theme. They just have to be special preparations that you do better than anyone else . . . and that your guests rave about. For example, locals know San Francisco's Tadich Grill as much for its creamed spinach as for its fish.

Appendix

Barry Cohen

Barry Cohen leads the foodservice industry in creating cutting-edge marketing strategies and management techniques. His "W.O.W." system is the first program to develop high-energy management into a discipline. His book, ***W.O.W. 2000***, has sold thousands of copies and his speeches draw crowds around the country.

He counts more than twenty years in the restaurant industry and has managed multi-unit, high-volume chains in Florida and Texas. He joined Old San Francisco Corporation as General Manager for the San Antonio restaurant in 1989. Four years later he became CEO. Old San Francisco now has restaurants in Austin, Dallas, Houston, San Antonio and Las Vegas.

Along with his corporate duties and speaking assignments, Barry is a frequent guest chef on local and national television programs and a regular guest host on local radio morning shows. He is an innovative epicurean who has received numerous awards for his recipes and has placed in the Great Chefs of Texas competition.

Barry received the coveted Pinnacle Award from the Sales and Marketing Executives of San Antonio, as well as the 1996 "Shoe Leather Marketer of the Year" Award from Restaurant Marketing, an influential industry newsletter. He has also written columns on W.O.W. for internationally known publications such as the Cornell University Quarterly and Nation's Restaurant News.

For more information, contact Barry Cohen at:

OLD SAN FRANCISCO STEAK HOUSE
9809 McCullough · San Antonio, TX 78216
Voice: (210) 341-3189 · FAX: (210) 341-3585
e-mail: osfcorp@onr.com
Internet website: www.osfsteakhouse.com

. . . or circle the following numbers on the reply card:
Consulting information: (05) **Speaking information: (06)**

Howard Cutson, FMP

Howard Cutson, FMP, is Principal of Cutson Associates, a customer satisfaction-oriented consulting firm serving the hospitality industry. He has spent more than 30 years working in all aspects of this industry - from bartender to maitre 'd and from Assistant Manager to Director of Marketing - giving him hands-on knowledge of the daily challenges of his clients.

He is a former Vice President of Stouffer Restaurant Company and faculty member at the University of Akron, teaching hospitality management and beverage management courses. He consults in the commercial restaurant/hotel sector as well as with private clubs, health care and B&I foodservice. Howard is the author of ***Hospitality Role-Play Trainer®,*** a unique program to improve the effectiveness of daily wait staff training.

His available workshops and presentations include:

Full-Day Workshops
- People Management 101
- Building Your Own All-Star Team
- Managing Today's Bar
- Taking Control of Turnover

Half-Day and Show-Length Programs
- Effective Bar Cost Controls
- Building Your Bar Sales
- Growing Lifetime Customers
- Building Employee Loyalty
- Doin' the Old Soft Sell
- Basics of Bar Hospitality
- Professional Telephone Skills

For more information, contact Howard Cutson at:

CUTSON ASSOCIATES
589 Atterbury Blvd. · Hudson, OH 44236
Voice/FAX: (216) 656-3335

. . . or circle the following numbers on the reply card:
Consulting information: (07) **Speaking information: (08)**

Peter Good, FMP

Peter Good is founder and Principal of Peter Good Seminars, Inc., a training company primarily serving the hospitality industry.

Peter combines his background as an educator and trainer with more than 20 years of restaurant operations experience in casual and fine dining settings. As Director of Education for the Illinois Restaurant Association, he designed and conducted seminar programs addressing topics critical to foodservice success including customer service, employee supervision and motivation, food safety, recruitment and hiring.

He is author of the forthcoming book, ***The MAGIC of Hospitality*** and a highly-regarded speaker for both his information and his inspirational messages. Peter's humorous and enthusiastic approach has earned him a reputation as one of the industry's most dynamic, motivational speakers. A frequent speaker for the National Restaurant Association's Educational Foundation, his audiences include McDonald's Corporation, Sysco Corporation, Divi Hotels & Resorts and TGI Friday's.

Peter is the recipient of the Distinguished Service award from the National Institute for the Foodservice Industry. He has been designated a Foodservice Management Professional by the Educational Foundation of the National Restaurant Association and is a member of the Professional Speakers of Illinois.

For additional information, contact Peter Good at:

PETER GOOD SEMINARS, INC.
14 W. Burlington, Suite 200
LaGrange, IL 60525
Voice: (800) 528-2190 · FAX: (708) 352-6767
e-mail: PeterGoodSem@earthlink.net

. . . or circle the following numbers on the reply card
Consulting information: (11) **Speaking information: (12)**

Raymond Goodman, PhD

Raymond Goodman is a Professor in the Department of Hospitality Management at the University of New Hampshire. He has been visiting faculty at the leading hospitality education institutions in the U.S. and Europe. He holds a Doctorate and Master's Degree from the School of Hotel Administration at Cornell University.

His has written books on the management and psychology of service (see recommended reading) and authored several articles for the Hospitality Industry trade press as well as in academic publications such as the Cornell Quarterly.

He is a member of the Council of Hotel and Restaurant Trainers (CHART), the American Hotel and Motel Association; the National Restaurant Association and the Council for Hotel, Restaurant and Institutional Educators (CHRIE). He is often a featured speaker for the American Hotel and Motel Association, the National Restaurant Association and numerous state lodging and restaurant associations.

Dr. Goodman provides a range of consulting services to food service institutions, chain and independent restaurants and long term care/retirement organizations. He works on an ongoing basis with Andrew Young and Company, an international restaurant concept/design firm.

For more information, contact Raymond Goodman at:

RAYMOND GOODMAN ASSOCIATES
PO Box 898, 4 Falls Way
Durham, NH 03824
Voice: (603) 659-3321 · FAX: (603) 659-4401
e-mail: RayGoodman@aol.com

. . . or circle the following numbers on the reply card:
Consulting information: (25) **Speaking information: (26)**

Jim Laube, CPA

Jim Laube is president of the Center for Foodservice Education in Houston, Texas. In his many seminars and workshops, Jim integrates the financial and operational sides of the business to provide practical, proven methods to help foodservice organizations operate more efficiently and more profitably.

Jim began his foodservice career at the age of 15 working for a quick-service restaurant and earned his way through college as a server and bartender. After college, he spent two years with a national accounting firm, then five years with a regional restaurant chain. He has held responsible positions in both the financial and operational sides of the business.

Since 1993, Jim has presented to thousands of foodservice professionals nationwide. His clients include Walt Disney, Popeye's Chicken & Biscuits, Harrah's Hotels, Vail Resorts and the Society for Foodservice Management. He is a personable, engaging speaker and earns high marks from audiences for his knowledge of the industry and the enthusiasm, clarity and personal experiences he incorporates into his programs.

Full Day Programs
- How to Improve Restaurant & Foodservice Profitability
- What Every Foodservice Pro Should Know About Improving Financial Management & Controls

Half Day and Show Programs
- Profit or Loss: Are You Managing the Financial Side of Your Restaurant?
- Ammunition to Win the Food Cost War

For more information, contact Jim Laube at:

CENTER FOR FOODSERVICE EDUCATION
9801 Westheimer, Suite 302 · Houston, Texas 77042
Voice: (888) 233-3555 · Fax: (888) 233-3777
e-mail: cfejsl@aol.com · website: www.cfeonline.com

. . . or circle the following numbers on the reply card:
Consulting information: (13) **Speaking information: (14)**

Bill Main, FMP, FCSI, CSP

Bill Main has a restaurant management company. He speaks throughout the United States and Canada. He consults on restaurant strategic planning, profitability and marketing. He writes regularly for several national trade magazines. He is a dedicated member of the historic Chaine des Rotisseurs and the Past President of the California Restaurant Association. Whew!

A fifth generation Californian, he earned his bachelor's degree in economics at Oregon State University. He was a three-year All-Pac-8 halfback and draft choice for the Pittsburgh Steelers. After a brief stint as a pro, he moved from the gridiron to the grill, starting at the famed Henry Africa's in San Francisco. After a year as food and beverage director at the McKinley Park Hotel in Alaska, in 1974 he formed Oceanshore Restaurants, Inc., a restaurant management company offering a full range of services including financial and marketing consulting.

Bill is a Certified Speaking Professional (CSP) in the National Speaker's Association and gives more than 80 presentations a year. Bill and his partner, Barbara Geshekter, have written three best-selling books on training and management. He is also a foodservice management consultant specializing in profit improvement and strategic planning. He is a member and past director of the Foodservice Consultants Society International (FCSI) and has been a visiting instructor at Cal Poly Pomona and the University of San Francisco.

For more information, contact Bill Main at:

BILL MAIN & ASSOCIATES
2220 St. George Lane, Suite 1
Chico, CA 95926
Voice: (800) 858-7876 · FAX: (916) 345-0212
e-mail: billmain@aol.com

. . . or circle the following numbers on the reply card:
Consulting information: (15) **Speaking information: (16)**

Phyllis Ann Marshall, FCSI

Phyllis Ann Marshall, Principal of FoodPower, has been a food industry consultant since 1978, involved with restaurant concepting and operational analysis. Her firm, FoodPower, specializes in growth strategies for quick-service and multi-unit operators. FoodPower provides seminars for restaurant operators, shopping center marketing directors and commercial property investors. Topics include Leadership Skills, Trends Review, Profitability, Team-Building, Profitability, Menu Marketing and Merchandising.

As co-owner and operator of Mr. Stox, one of Southern California's most popular restaurants, she helped create an innovative and highly-regarded dining facility which has received top industry awards. She is a frequent contributor to national restaurant and food-related trade publications and is the restaurant reviewer for Orange Coast magazine. She is an advisor to the University of California Irvine in the development of a Restaurant Management Certificate Program.

Phyllis Ann holds a degree in Food and Nutrition from Cornell University. She trained in Paris at La Varenne Ecole de Cuisine, in London at Le Cordon Bleu, with chefs in Hong Kong, Madrid, Florence and Nice and with Julia Child in the U.S.. Phyllis Ann is a member of Chaine des Rotisseurs and the Foodservice Consultants Society International (FCSI). She is certified by the Association of Culinary Professionals and is a founding member of the Association of Women Chefs and Restaurateurs.

For more information, contact Phyllis Ann Marshall at:

FOODPOWER
2463 Irvine Ave., Suite E-1
Costa Mesa, CA 92627
Voice: (714) 646-3206 · FAX: (714) 646-1390
e-mail: foodpower@aol.com

. . . or circle the following numbers on the reply card:
Consulting information: (17) **Speaking information: (18)**

Bill Marvin
The Restaurant Doctor™

Bill Marvin, the most-booked speaker in the hospitality business, is an advisor to service-oriented companies across North America. Bill founded **Effortless, Inc.**, a management research and education company, **Prototype Restaurants**, a hospitality consulting group and the **Hospitality Masters Press.**

Bill started his working life at the age of 14, washing dishes (by hand!) in a small restaurant on Cape Cod and went on to earn a degree in Hotel Administration from Cornell University. A veteran of the foodservice industry, Bill has managed hotels, institutions and clubs and owned full service restaurants. He has had the keys in his hand, his name on the loans and the payrolls to meet. His professional curiosity and practical experience enable him to grasp (and teach) the human factors common to the growth and success of every type of hospitality enterprise.

He is a member of the Council of Hotel and Restaurant Trainers (CHART) and the National Speakers Association. He has achieved all major professional certifications in the foodservice industry. He is a prolific author, a featured guest on Hospitality Television and is a regular columnist in the trade journals of several industries. In addition to his private consulting practice, he logs over 150,000 miles a year delivering corporate keynote addresses and conducting staff and management training programs in the U.S., Canada, Ireland and other international venues.

For more information, contact Bill Marvin at:

EFFORTLESS, INC.
PO Box 280 · Gig Harbor, WA 98335
Voice: (800) 767-1055 · FAX: (888) 767-1055
e-mail: bill@restaurantdoctor.com
website: www.restaurantdoctor.com

. . . or circle the following numbers on the reply card:
Consulting information: (19) **Speaking information: (20)**

Banger Smith

Banger Smith is founder and principal of Menus for Profit, a front-runner in the field of menu analysis, engineering, design and merchandising. He has helped hundreds of restaurateurs across the country achieve greater profitability through his knowledge of menu merchandising and point of purchase collateral and has been hailed as the "miracle worker of menus."

Banger is quick to point out that even the best menu cannot replace a well-trained and knowledgeable service staff. But he's proven that with a menu and related merchandising materials that take full advantage of their marketing potential, and a sales staff working to sell the right items, profits will skyrocket. His unique approach to menus has helped his clients increase gross profits as much as 12% per month per store.

Banger is a restaurant management veteran with more than 20 years in the business. He served nine years as General Manager with nationally acclaimed, Ray's Boathouse in Seattle. Before he started Menus for Profit in early 1996, he was Vice President of The Menu Workshop in Seattle, working miracles for both large and small restaurant companies throughout the U.S. and Canada.

His clients include Red Lobster, Consolidated Restaurants, Dave & Busters, Holland America Line, Harrah's Casinos, Chevy's Mexican Restaurants, Noble House Hotels, El Gaucho, White Spot Restaurants, Andaluca and Metropolitan Grill.

For more information, contact Banger Smith at:

MENUS FOR PROFIT
100 W. Harrison Street, Suite 530 · Seattle, WA 98119
Voice: (800) 637-6368 · Fax: (206) 284-5433
e-mail: banger@menusforprofit.com
Internet website: www.menusforprofit.com

. . . or circle the following numbers on the reply card:
Consulting information: (29) **Speaking information: (30)**

Ron Yudd

Ron Yudd is an experienced speaker, trainer and motivator with over twenty-five years of operational experience in the restaurant industry. He is Director of Food Service for the United States Senate, where he has worked since 1978. In his duties at the Senate Restaurants, he directs more than 250 staff members serving more than 12,000 meals per day in 14 different restaurants. Sixty percent of the Senate's $8 million in annual foodservice sales is generated from special events and catering.

Ron began teaching foodservice management courses in 1980 at local colleges and culinary schools. In 1986 he became an international instructor for the Educational Foundation of the National Restaurant Association. He continues to travel and teach a variety of profit and service-oriented courses.

As a keynote speaker, Ron has addressed prominent national and international groups on profitability, passion for quality service, training the service employee and service leadership. He combines a motivating style with practical take-home ideas that have immediate application on the job. Ron's most requested presentations include:

- A Passion for Service: Managing for the Guest
- Points of Profit: Cost-Effective Operations
- Personal and Professional Success for the Foodservice Operator

Ron is author of ***Successful Buffet Management,*** a textbook used extensively by chefs and catering managers, and is working on two exciting new books, ***A Passion for Service*** to be followed by ***Points of Profit***

For more information, contact Ron Yudd at:

10181 Nightingale Street
Gaithersburg, MD 20882
Voice/FAX: (301) 253-4728

. . . or circle the following numbers on the reply card:
Consulting information: (23) **Speaking information: (24)**

RECOMMENDED READING

For readers who wish to improve their professional knowledge, we recommend these books by our contributing authors. For purchase information, please circle the numbers on the reader reply card or contact the authors directly.

Howard Cutson

(32) ***Hospitality Role-Play Trainer®,*** Cutson Associates

Peter Good

(48) ***The Magic of Hospitality***, 1998, Hospitality Masters Press

Raymond Goodman

(49) ***The Management of Service for the Restaurant Manager,*** 1996, Richard D. Irwin

Bill Main

(38) ***Profit Tools™ - Front of the House Series***

(39) ***Profit Tools™ - Back of the House Series***

(40) ***Profit Tools™ - Top of the House Series***

(50) ***Menu Magic™***

(71) ***Selling Solutions - Redefining Value Instead of Negotiating Price***

(72) ***Marketing Backward - Strategic Planning for 2005***

(73) ***Management Recruiting & Hiring Protocols***

Bill Marvin

(41) ***Restaurant Basics: Why Guests Don't Come Back and What You Can Do About It***, 1992, John Wiley & Sons, Inc.

(42) ***The Foolproof Foodservice Selection System: The Complete Manual for Creating a Quality Staff,*** 1993, John Wiley & Sons

(43) ***From Turnover to Teamwork: How to Build and Retain a Customer-Oriented Foodservice Staff,*** 1994, John Wiley & Sons

(44) ***50 Tips to Improve Your Tips: The Service Pro's Guide to Delighting Diners,*** 1997, Hospitality Masters Press

(45) ***Guest-Based Marketing: How to Increase Restaurant Sales Without Breaking Your Budget***, 1997, John Wiley & Sons

(46) ***Cashing in on Complaints: Turning Disappointed Diners into Gold,*** 1997, Hospitality Masters Press

Ron Yudd

(47) ***Successful Buffet Management,*** 1990, Van Nostrand Reinhold

OFFERS YOU CAN'T REFUSE!

Our contributing authors are pleased to provide you with even more value by offering something for nothing! To request any of the information described below, just circle the corresponding number on the reader reply card or write directly to the author. (Note: SASE="self-addressed, stamped envelope.")

From Barry Cohen

To help you create a "WOW" environment that will energize you, your staff and your guests, get a free copy of Barry's checklist, ***Ten Points to "WOW" Yourself.*** Circle **56** or send a SASE to Barry Cohen, Old San Francisco Steak House, 9809 McCullough, San Antonio, TX 78216.

From Howard Cutson

Want to build stronger beverage sales? Get a free copy of Howard Cutson's **Recipe for Developing Specialty Drinks that Really Sell!** Circle **83** or send a SASE to Cutson Associates, 589 Atterbury Blvd., Hudson, OH 44236 and start improving your bar and lounge sales today!

From Peter Good

Take a positive step toward happier patrons with a free copy of ***Five Steps to Memorable Guest Service.*** Circle **60** or send a SASE to Peter Good Seminars, 14 W. Burlington, #200, LaGrange, IL 60525.

From Raymond Goodman

Everybody is aware of sanitation in the kitchen, but how about the dining room? To get a handle on this critical area, Circle **75** or send a SASE to Raymond Goodman, PO Box 898, Durham, NH 03824 for a free copy of his ***Dining Room Sanitation Checklist.***

Have you looked at your Workers Comp and liability premiums lately? Don't take risks you can avoid. For a free copy of his ***Dining Room Safety Checklist,*** circle **76** or send a SASE to Raymond Goodman, PO Box 898, Durham, NH 03824.

Your staff can never be to well-trained. To receive a free copy of Raymond's ***Food & Beverage Terminology Checklist for Server Training,*** circle **77** or send a SASE to Raymond Goodman, PO Box 898, Durham, NH 03824.

From Jim Laube

How well are you managing the financial side of your restaurant? Compare yourself with techniques used by the industry's most successful restaurateurs. For a free copy of ***The Restaurant Operators Financial IQ Checklist,*** circle **61** or send a SASE.

Are common foodservice misconceptions costing you money? To find out, get a free copy of ***The Top 10 Myths of Foodservice Profitability.*** Circle **62** or send a SASE to Center For Foodservice Education, 9801 Westheimer, Suite 302, Houston, TX 77042.

From Bill Main

Want a little help to get you started on building your menu profits? Circle **84** or send a SASE to Bill Main & Associates, 2231 St. George Lane, Suite 10, Chico, CA 959226 for a copy of Bill's ***Menu Item Costing Worksheet.***

From Phyllis Ann Marshall

Would you like to gain an edge over your competitors and make your restaurant more marketable? Circle **63** or send a SASE for a copy of ***Becoming a Brand – the Secret to an Unfair Advantage*** to FoodPower, 2463 Irvine Ave., Ste E-1, Costa Mesa, CA 92627.

From Bill Marvin, The Restaurant Doctor™

If you agree that the key to implementing a good menu is a good staff, ask for a free copy of Bill's audio tape ***Selecting Service-Oriented People***. Circle **85** or send a SASE to Effortless, Inc., PO Box 280, Gig Harbor, WA 98335.

To assess your level of guest service, ask for a free copy of Bill's ***Guest Service Self-Evaluation Checklist.*** Circle **80** or send a SASE to Effortless, Inc., PO Box 280, Gig Harbor, WA 98335.

Six times a year, Bill publishes the ***Home Remedies Newsletter***, full of practical insights for managers. The subscription is $24 but he will send you a year for free . . . if you ask! Circle **66** or send a request to Effortless, Inc., PO Box 280, Gig Harbor, WA 98335.

From Banger Smith

Let Menus for Profit perform a mini menu analysis and critique of your menu merchandising program – you'll receive profit-making ideas that can boost your average gross profit as much as 15%! Send your menu(s) along with one period's sales mix with recipe costs and Banger will do the rest. Circle **81** for more information or send your material to Menus for Profit, 100 W. Harrison Street, Suite 530, Seattle, WA 98119.

Don't continue to use an unprofitable menu. Get Banger's free report, ***The Top Ten Reasons to Change Your Menu.*** Circle **82** or send a SASE to Menus for Profit, 100 W. Harrison Street, Suite 530, Seattle, WA 98119.

From Ron Yudd

Jump-start your guests' satisfaction with a copy of the handout from Ron's acclaimed seminar, ***A Passion for Service.*** Circle **68** or send a SASE to Ron Yudd at 10181 Nightingale Street, Gaithersburg, MD 20882.

Tested ideas from the leading speakers and consultants in the hospitality industry

Other books in the Hospitality Masters Series:

50 Proven Ways to Build Restaurant Sales & Profit
50 Proven Ways to Enhance Guest Service

Did you borrow this book? Do you want a copy of your own? Do you need extra copies for your staff and management? Do you want to take advantage of the incredible free offers from the contributing authors?

BOOK ORDER

YES! I want to invest in my future success and have personal copies of the following books in the Hospitality Masters Series:

______ ***50 Proven Ways to Build Restaurant Sales & Profit***
______ ***50 Proven Ways to Build More Profitable Menus***
______ ***50 Proven Ways to Enhance Guest Service***

1-14 copies: $14.95 each plus postage & handling*
15+ copies: call for discount information

POSTAGE & HANDLING
MUST BE ADDED TO ALL ORDERS
Figure postage & handling at the greater of $5.00* or 6% of the total book order.

Total No. Copies __________

Total Amount of Order: $ __________

Method of Payment: ☐ Check ☐ Money Order ☐ VISA ☐ MC ☐ Amex

Account No. ____________________

Expires _______ **Signature** ____________________

*Canadian funds: $19.95 + postage & handling (greater of $6.00 or 8% of book order)
Allow 30 days for delivery on all orders

return to:

HOSPITALITY MASTERS PRESS
PO Box 280 • Gig Harbor, WA 98335

For faster service, FAX your request toll-free to (888) 767-1055

FREE OFFERS AND INFORMATION

Use this form to find out more about the contributing authors to this book or to request the free material offered in Appendix C. Allow 30 days for delivery.

01	02	03	04	05	06	07	08	09	10
11	12	13	14	15	16	17	18	19	20
21	22	23	24	25	26	27	28	29	30
31	32	33	34	35	36	37	38	39	40
41	42	43	44	45	46	47	48	49	50
51	52	53	54	55	56	57	58	58	60
61	62	63	64	65	66	67	68	69	70
71	72	73	74	75	76	77	78	79	80
81	82	83	84	85	86	87	88	89	90

SEND BOOKS AND INFORMATION TO:

Name ____________________

Company ____________________

Address ____________________

City ____________ **State** _____ **Zip** _______

Phone ____________ **Fax** ____________

e-mail ____________________